LATIN *FOR THE* NEW MILLENNIUM

LATIN 3

SELECT LATIN
ENRICHMENT READINGS

LATIN FOR THE NEW MILLENNIUM
Series Information

LEVEL ONE
Student Text, Second Edition
Student Workbook, Second Edition
College Exercise Book, Levels 1 and 2
Teacher's Manual, Second Edition
Teacher's Manual for Student Workbook, Second Edition

ENRICHMENT TEXTS
From Romulus to Romulus Augustulus:
Roman History for the New Millennium
The Original Dysfunctional Family:
Basic Classical Mythology for the New Millennium

LEVEL TWO
Student Text, Second Edition
Student Workbook, Second Edition
Teacher's Manual, Second Edition
Teacher's Manual for Student Workbook, Second Edition

ENRICHMENT TEXTS
From Rome to Reformation:
Early European History for the New Millennium
The Clay-footed SuperHeroes:
Mythology Tales for the New Millennium

LEVEL THREE
Student Text
Teacher's Manual

ENRICHMENT TEXTS
Latin 3: Select Latin Enrichment Readings

ELECTRONIC RESOURCES
www.lnm.bolchazy.com
www.bolchazy.com/ebooks.htm
Quia Question Bank

LATIN *FOR THE* NEW MILLENNIUM

LATIN 3

SELECT LATIN ENRICHMENT READINGS

Edited by Helena Dettmer and LeaAnn A. Osburn

Bolchazy-Carducci Publishers, Inc.

Mundelein, Illinois USA

Series Editor: LeaAnn A. Osburn

Volume Editor: Bridget Dean

Contributing Editors: Laurel Draper, Donald Sprague

Design & Layout: Adam Phillip Velez

Cover Illustration: The Dying Gaul. Marble replica of one of the sculptures in the ex-voto group dedicated to Pergamon by Attalus I to commemorate the victories over the Galatians in the 3rd and 2nd centuries BCE. Capitoline Museums, Rome. (© Wikimedia Commons)

Latin for the New Millennium
Latin 3: Select Latin Enrichment Readings

Helena Dettmer and LeaAnn A. Osburn, Editors

Bolchazy-Carducci Publishers, Inc.
1570 Baskin Road
Mundelein, Illinois 60060
www.bolchazy.com

Printed in the United States of America
2017
by United Graphics

ISBN 978-0-86516-797-1

Library of Congress Cataloging-in-Publication Data

Select Latin enrichment readings / edited by Helena Dettmer and LeaAnn A. Osburn. -- First edition.
    pages cm -- (Latin for the new millennium ; 3)
  Includes bibliographical references and index.
  ISBN 978-0-86516-797-1 (pbk. : alk. paper) 1. Latin literature. I. Dettmer, Helena. II. Osburn,
LeaAnn A. III. Series: Latin for the new millennium ; 3.
  PA6116.S45 2013
  870.8'001--dc23

                                                                                    2013017828

Dedicated to Lou Bolchazy

for his vast contributions to the study
of the Classical languages

for his unswerving devotion to providing
what classicists need in their classroom

for his own unique way of making
each conference a little better

for making us all see what it means
to promote the study of Classics

and most of all

for mentoring so many of us in ways great and small

CONTENTS

LIST OF MAPS

LIST OF IMAGES

PREFACE

This text serves a dual purpose of complementing the readings and material found in *Latin for the New Millennium*, Level 3, and of providing an intermediate reader of interesting passages for students who have learned from any introductory Latin text. Plentiful vocabulary and notes accompany the passages in order to enable students to focus on reading unadapted Latin. Students should read the introductions to each author, which set the author and his writings in the appropriate historical milieu. A short set of comprehension questions follows each reading and will allow students to see how well they have understood the passage. End matter includes a section on Latin Meters, a section on Rhetorical Terms, and a Latin to English glossary.

Some figures of speech (printed in small caps) are identified in notes to the Latin passages. Students should read the text carefully in order to identify other figures of speech and to determine for themselves how the author's use of a particular figure of speech enhances the line, sentence, or passage.

The meter is noted at the beginning of a poetic selection. Students are encouraged to use Appendix A to help them scan lines from any poem in this reader. Scanning Latin poetry will allow students to have a guide for how to read the poetry aloud, observing the poetic rhythm.

This text enables students to recognize literary interplay between Latin authors. As a result, it provides a glimpse into the culture of the classical period and into the dynamics between contemporary authors such as Vergil and Horace, and Catullus and Cicero, and between Baroque authors and their famous classical predecessors.

Vergil and Horace both belonged to the literary circle of Maecenas, who served as patron to leading poets of the day. Vergil, in fact, was responsible for introducing Horace to their common benefactor. Horace addressed three of his odes to Vergil (1.3, 1.24, and 4.12), and their close relationship is particularly clear from *Odes* 1.3 (p. 82), where Horace describes his friend "as half of his soul."

Catullus addresses one of his poems to Cicero (Poem 49). In this poem he imitates Cicero's penchant for using superlative adjectives. Five superlative adjectives occur in the space of seven lines, and there is one instance of anaphora, another favorite stylistic device of Cicero's.

Catullus was friends with Cicero's protégé, Marcus Caelius Rufus. In Catullus's Poem 77 we discover that Caelius "stole" Lesbia (Clodia) from Catullus. Clodia looms large in Cicero's *Prō Caeliō*. Attacking Clodia in his speech on Caelius's behalf, Cicero suggests the motive behind her, in his view, false accusations that Caelius stole gold from her and attempted to poison her: she was avenging herself on Caelius for breaking off their love affair. In his bitter poem to his faithless friend Rufus (Poem 77), Catullus refers to the second accusation by Clodia (Lesbia) by addressing Rufus as a "cruel poison" (*heu heu nostrae crūdēle venēnum / vītae, heu heu nostrae pestis amīcitiae*).

Cicero and Caesar knew each other well since they were contemporaries; both served in the Roman Senate, and both were elected consuls. They were further connected through Cicero's brother Quintus, who served with Caesar in Gaul. Caesar was a master politician; Cicero Rome's most brilliant orator. They did not see eye to eye on the future of the Republic. Cicero was a traditionalist and clung to the notion of preserving the *rēs pūblica*, of keeping it the way it was. Caesar recognized that that form of government was antiquated. Caesar was right. But, in the end, both died similarly and violently, at the hands of their enemies.

Ovid was born in the year 43 BCE. Since he lived a generation later than Vergil and Horace, he was influenced by his Latin predecessors of that period (including the poets Propertius and Tibullus whose works are not included in this text). Ovid's greatest work was his *Metamorphōsēs*, in which he was heavily indebted to Vergil in terms of epic technique and language. Many see his *Metamorphōsēs* as written largely in response to Vergil's *Aeneid*.

To be well educated in the Baroque period meant reading and knowing well Latin and Greek authors. The two late Baroque writers Lieven De Meyere and Mathias Casimir Sarbiewski were influenced by classical authors just as classical authors influenced each other. This text includes one poem from each of these Baroque writers to illustrate the continuity of the classical tradition.

# ACKNOWLEDGEMENTS

The author-editors would like to thank the many individuals who have offered us help through personal comments and written suggestions as well as those who have assisted in our completing this reader in a timely manner, including:

Our editors, Bridget Dean and Donald Sprague, for all their suggestions and comments from the inception of this project;

The College of Liberal Arts and Sciences at the University of Iowa for generously providing funds for Billie Cotterman, Jackie Jones, and Joshua Langseth, graduate students at the University, to augment the vocabulary for several authors and to Joshua Langseth for his assistance in closely proofreading the text;

Donald Sprague and Karrie Singh for their careful work on the Post-antique Writers section;

and all the authors whose books previously published by Bolchazy-Carducci Publishers have formed sections of this book including Ronnie Ancona, Henry Bender, Barbara Weiden Boyd, Stephen Ciraolo, Phyllis Young Forsyth, Jozef IJsewijn, Charbra Adams Jestin, Phyllis Katz, James J. Mertz, SJ, Hans-Friedrich Mueller, John P. Murphy, SJ, Tom Sienkewicz, and Rose Williams.

We would like to recognize, too, Terry Stone and Mark Ducar Sr., who provided moral support through this lengthy project, and, especially, the late Lou Bolchazy, to whom we dedicate this reader, for his vision that this series with all its components was truly needed.

WORKS CONSULTED, ADAPTED, AND REVISED

These titles are those Bolchazy-Carducci texts that were adapted and revised for *Latin for the New Millennium*, Level 3. The editors adapted translations and answers from the teacher guides and teacher manuals that appear in this list.

CAESAR

Mueller, Hans-Friedrich. *Caesar: Selections from His COMMENTARII DE BELLO GALLICO*. Mundelein, IL: Bolchazy-Carducci Publishers, 2012.

CATULLUS

Bender, Henry V., and Phyllis Young Forsyth. *Catullus Expanded Edition*. Wauconda, IL: Bolchazy-Carducci Publishers, 2008.

———. *Catullus: Expanded Edition Teacher's Guide*. Wauconda, IL: Bolchazy-Carducci Publishers, 2007.

CICERO

Ciraolo, Stephen. *Cicero: PRO CAELIO*. Mundelein, IL: Bolchazy-Carducci Publishers, 2003.

HORACE

Ancona, Ronnie. *Horace: Selected ODES and SATIRE 1.9*, 2nd ed. Wauconda, IL: Bolchazy-Carducci Publishers, 2005.

———. *Horace: Selected ODES and SATIRE 1.9, Teacher's Guide*, 2nd ed. Wauconda, IL: Bolchazy-Carducci Publishers, 2005.

OVID

———. *Ovid: AMORES, METAMORPHOSES Selections*, 2nd ed. Wauconda, IL: Bolchazy-Carducci Publishers, 2000.

POST-ANTIQUE LATIN

Mertz, James J., SJ, Jozef IJsewijn and John P. Murphy. *Jesuit Latin Poets of the 17th and 18th Centuries*. Wauconda, IL: Bolchazy-Carducci Publishers, 1989.

VERGIL

Boyd, Barbara Weiden. *Vergil's AENEID: Selections from Books 1, 2, 4, 6, 10, & 12*. Wauconda, IL: Bolchazy-Carducci Publishers, 2002.

———. *Vergil's AENEID: Selections from Books 1, 2, 4, 6, 10, & 12, Teacher's Guide*. Wauconda, IL: Bolchazy-Carducci Publishers, 2002.

# GENERAL EDITORS AND CONTRIBUTORS

HELENA DETTMER

BA Indiana University; PhD University of Michigan

Professor of Classics and Associate Dean for Undergraduate Programs in the College of Liberal Arts and Sciences at the University of Iowa

Dettmer received the University of Iowa's 2012 Lola Lopes Award for Undergraduate Student Advocacy. A former Mellon Fellow at Duke University, a recipient of the Iowa May Brodbeck Humanities Fellowship, an Iowa Faculty Scholar, an Iowa collegiate fellow, and past president of the Classical Association of the Middle West and South, Dettmer has authored *Horace: A Study in Structure* (1983) and *Love by the Numbers: Form and Meaning in the Poetry of Catullus* (1997). She is coauthor of *A Workbook to Ayers' English Words from Latin and Greek Elements* (1986), in its second printing and used widely in vocabulary-building courses around the country, as well as *A Catullus Workbook* (2006) and its *Teacher's Manual* (2006), which she coauthored with LeaAnn Osburn. Her current project is a book-length study examining the poetic structure of Ovid's *Amores*.

LEAANN A. OSBURN

BA Monmouth College, Illinois; MA Loyola University Chicago

Teacher Emerita, Barrington High School, Barrington, Illinois

LeaAnn A. Osburn received an American Classical League *Emerita* Award in 2012, served as both vice president and president of the Illinois Classical Conference, and received the ICC Lifetime Achievement Award in 2008. Osburn received the Illinois Latin Teacher of the

Year Award (1989), the Illinois Lt. Governor's Award (1990), and the CAMWS Good Teacher Award (1996). She coauthored *A Catullus Workbook* (2006) and *Teacher's Manual* (2006) with Helena Dettmer, *Vergil: A Legamus Transitional Reader* (2004) with Thomas J. Sienkewicz, and *Vergil: A Legamus Transitional Reader Teacher's Guide* (2010) with Karen Lee Singh. Osburn served as the series editor for *Latin for the New Millennium*, Levels 1 and 2.

# INTRODUCTION

This supplementary reader provides authentic Latin passages from major authors of the Republic and Augustan periods, with a final section containing authors from the Baroque period. These authors include Caesar, Catullus, Cicero, Vergil, Horace, Ovid, Lieven De Meyere, and Mathias Casimir Sarbiewski. Succinct summaries of the Latin passages contained in the text follow, with suggestions of how these supplemental readings might be paired with Latin that the students either have read or could be assigned to read.

READINGS

CAESAR

Dē bellō Cīvīlī 3.103–104 (Readings 3 and 4) relate how Pompey the Great, hoping to receive asylum from King Ptolemy of Egypt after he was defeated by Caesar in the battle of Pharsalus, instead met his death as a result of Egyptian treachery. These passages from *Dē bellō Cīvīlī* could be read in conjunction with *Aeneid* 2.557–558 (p. 268, LNM 3); there Vergil describes the end of Priam, whose brutal death may have been modeled after that of Pompey.

The other passages from Caesar, *Dē bellō Gallicō* 6.13–16, provide fascinating cultural material on the Druids, which students are certain to enjoy reading. The Druid passages show an ethnographical style of reporting that contrasts well with Caesar's writings about war and strategy as in Book 1 of his *Dē bellō Gallicō* (pp. 18–76, LNM 3) or in Readings 3 and 4 in this reader from *Dē bellō Cīvīlī*.

CATULLUS

The section on Catullus includes four poems, all of them involving Lesbia either directly or indirectly. In Poem 11, one of Catullus's most famous Lesbia poems, the lover-poet announces to Lesbia through intermediaries that the affair is over. This poem often is read along with Poem 51 (pp. 118–120, *LNM* 3). Catullus clearly indicated a connection between Poems 11 and 51 by composing these poems, and only these poems, in the Sapphic meter.

Catullus 77 concerns friendship betrayed. It is likely that this poem is addressed to (Caelius) Rufus, who stole Lesbia/Clodia from Catullus and who, we learn from Cicero's *Prō Caeliō* in Readings 9 and 10, in turn incurred Lesbia's/Clodia's anger by breaking off the affair with her. By addressing Rufus as *venēnum* ("poison") here, Catullus subtly refers to one of the two charges that Cicero addresses in his speech on Caelius Rufus's behalf, the charge that Caelius attempted to poison Clodia/Lesbia.

There are many poems in the Catullan corpus concerned with Lesbia, but only two are exuberantly happy, Poem 5 (pp. 92–94 in *LNM* 3) and Poem 107. Poem 5 has as its subject the euphoria of passionate love; poem 107, Reading 6, the euphoria of an unexpected reconciliation. In both instances the unadulterated joy is conveyed by verbal repetition. Although Reading 7, Poem 109, deals also with the theme of reconciliation, the tone of this poem is measured. The reader is to assume that some time has elapsed between the dramatic situation in the two poems and reality has set in. By this point in the collection (Poem 109 is the final Lesbia poem), Catullus the lover-poet knows, and the reader knows, that Lesbia is incapable of being true to him, no matter what she promises.

CICERO

The selections from Cicero come from his *Prō Caeliō*, 13 and 14.33–34. These passages focus on the role of Clodia (who many scholars believe was Catullus's Lesbia) in the prosecution of Caelius Rufus. Cicero's characterization of Clodia here corresponds to the unflattering picture that Catullus paints of Lesbia in Poems 11 (Reading 5), 37, and 58 as promiscuous ("striking up most shameful love affairs" *Prō Caeliō*, 14.33–34, line 28).

VERGIL

In *Aeneid* 6.14–41 (Reading 11) the engravings on the doors of the temple of Apollo succinctly convey the myth of Daedalus. This passage connects with Horace's allusion to Daedalus's daring escape from Crete in *Odes* 1.3.34–35 (Reading 14) and with Ovid's narrative in *Metamorphōsēs*, Book 8 (Reading 16) that describes the escape of Daedalus and Icarus, his son, from Crete.

Aeneid 6.450–476 (Reading 12) could be read in conjunction with Book 4, since it provides closure to the tragic love story of Dido and Aeneas (pp. 288–300, *LNM* 3). Here Aeneas meets Dido in the Underworld, where he learns that his former lover committed suicide in a desperate response to his departure.

Aeneid 6.847–866, 893–899 (Reading 13) tells how Aeneas left the underworld after a review of Roman heroes who are to be born. This passage (and lines that precede this passage) justify Aeneas's mission, to found the Latin race, and Rome's mission as well. This passage is important for the understanding of the *Aeneid* as a whole.

HORACE

Odes 1.3 (Reading 14) is a send-off poem for Vergil, who is making a voyage to Greece. The description of Vergil as "half of Horace's soul" suggests their close personal relationship. On a metaphorical level, the poem may refer to Horace's perception that Vergil is bold and daring in undertaking the project of the writing of his epic poem, the *Aeneid*. To put this in context, some of Vergil's contemporaries must have found it surprising that Vergil, who embraced the tenets of Callimachus and the neoterics regarding smallness of scope, would write a long continuous epic poem with Homer's *Iliad* and *Odyssey* as models.

Odes 1.22 (Reading 15) concerns the invulnerability of the virtuous lover-poet. The travelogue here is reminiscent of that in Catullus 11 (Reading 5), where Catullus enumerates the various dangerous places where Furius and Aurelius would be willing to accompany him. *Odes* 1.22 also recalls another Catullan poem through the phrase "sweetly laughing." *Dulce ridentem* deliberately echoes the same phrase used to describe Lesbia in Poem 51 (pp. 118–120, *LNM* 3). *Odes* 1.22 also might be profitably compared and contrasted with these Horatian love poems, *Odes* 1.5, 1.11, and 1.23, presented in *Latin for the New Millennium*, Level 3 (pp. 312–327).

OVID

In *Metamorphōsēs* Book 8.183–235 (Reading 16) the poignant tale of the death of Icarus recalls the similarly moving tale of the deaths of Pyramus and Thisbe, Book 4.65–166 (pp. 352–382, *LNM* 3): in both stories attempts to negotiate barriers have tragic consequences. Daedalus has in common with Pygmalion, Book 10.243–297 (pp. 390–404, *LNM* 3) that each is a gifted artist. The connection between the Daedalus and Pygmalion stories is further suggested by a verbal echo (cf. *Hymettia sōle / cēra remollēscit tractātaque pollice multās / flectitur infaciēs* 10.284–286 and *flāvam modo pollice cēram / mollībat* 8.198–199).

LIEVEN DE MEYERE

This poem in praise of Horace recalls *Odes* 2.10 (pp. 332–335, *LNM* 3) with its allusion to the golden mean (*aurea praecepta*) and *Odes* 3.30 (pp. 340–343, *LNM* 3) with its reference to Horace adapting Greek meters to Latin poetry. The allusion to Daedalus in line 13 connects the poem with all earlier references to Daedalus in this enrichment reader (Horace, *Odes* 1.3, Vergil, *Aeneid* Book 6, and Ovid, *Metamorphōsēs,* Book 8).

MATHIAS CASIMIR SARBIEWSKI

The second poem of Sarbiweski's *Liber Epodon* celebrates the spring *Sona.* Interestingly, the poem begins (*Fōns innocentī lūcidus magis vitrō*) by echoing the start of Horace's poem to the Bandusian spring (*Ō fōns Bandusiae, splendidior vitrō* 3.13.1), which Sarbiewski identifies near the end of the poem (line 19). Sarbiewski's poem also refers to Catullus's island retreat, Sirmio of Poem 31. Sarbiewski borrows from Catullus the notion that the site enables the physical restoration of the self. In addition, verbal reminiscences connect the two poems. *Ocelle nātālis solī* in 2.4 echoes *paene īnsulārum . . . īnsulārumque / ocelle* in 31.1–2, and *longīs viārum languidus labōribus* in 2.5 echoes *penegrinō / labōre fessī* in 31.8–9. The final line of Sarbiewski's poem explicitly makes mention of Sirmio.

SIGNS AND ABBREVIATIONS

abl. = ablative

acc. = accusative

adj. = adjective

adv. = adverb

card. = cardinal

cf. = Latin, *cōnfer*; English, "compare"

conj. = conjugation

dat. = dative

e.g. = Latin, *exemplī grātiā*; English, "for the sake of an example," usually reduced to "for example"

f. = feminine

ff. = and following

gen. = genitive

i.e. = Latin, *id est*; English, "that is"

indecl. = indeclinable

interj. = interjection

interrog. = interrogative

lit. = literally

m. = masculine

n. = neuter

num. = number

p. = page

pl. = plural

pp. = pages

prep. = preposition

pron. = pronoun

rel. = relative

CHAPTER 1

GAIUS JULIUS CAESAR

AN INTRODUCTION TO CAESAR

Gaius Julius Caesar is considered one of Rome's leading politicians (aedile in 65 BCE, *pontifex maximus* in 63, quaestor in 61, and consul in 59) and most successful generals. An accomplished orator, he also was an author of the first rank. His impact on Rome's political and religious institutions was decisive and long-lasting despite the fact that his life was cut short by his assassination in 44 BCE.

Caesar's literary fame rests on his surviving "commentaries" on the Gallic and Civil Wars: *Commentāriī dē bellō Gallicō* and *Commentāriī dē bellō Cīvīlī*. Caesar's actual reports to the Senate are not what we read today. We read reports modeled on the genre of those reports. When Caesar departed for Gaul, he probably chose *commentāriī* as a genre to publicize his accomplishments among as wide a public as possible in a format that made it appear as if he were sharing his official reports to the Senate with all Roman citizens. Similarly, Caesar's "reports" on the civil war were likely crucial in presenting Caesar's side in this bitterly divisive conflict.

Caesar's style has often been praised for its distinctive qualities. He tells his stories logically, clearly, and without obscure Latin vocabulary. Caesar also writes about himself in the third person. His intent in doing so has been the subject of scholarly debate. Caesar's *commentāriī* have persuaded many readers over thousands of years with this seemingly objective authority. A cursory glance, however, at the bitterly partisan times in which they appeared quickly reveals what was at stake for Caesar: his reputation, his public career, and even his life, as the subsequent civil war and Caesar's murder amply demonstrate.

READING 1

Caesar discusses the Druids in some detail in this passage, one of two groups that are respected among the Gauls.

THE DRUIDS AS PRIESTS AND ARBITRATORS

CAESAR *DĒ BELLŌ GALLICŌ* 6.13

1   [13] In omnī Galliā eōrum hominum quī aliquō sunt numerō
    atque honōre, genera sunt duo. Nam plēbēs paene servōrum
    habētur locō, quae nihil audet per sē, nūllō adhibētur cōnsiliō.
    Plērīque, cum aut aere aliēnō aut magnitūdine tribūtōrum aut

5   iniūriā potentiōrum premuntur, sēsē in servitūtem dicant
    nōbilibus, quibus in hōs eadem omnia sunt iūra quae dominīs in
    servōs. Sed dē hīs duōbus generibus alterum est druidum,
    alterum equitum. Illī rēbus dīvīnīs intersunt, sacrificia pūblica

NOTES AND VOCABULARY

Line 1:   **aliquis, aliquid** some, someone, anyone, something, anything

            numerus, -ī, m. account, number

Line 2:   **honōs, honōris,** m. mark of honor, office; honor, esteem; *numerō* and *honōre* are ablatives of description.

            genus, generis, n. type, kind

            nam, *conj.* for

            plēbēs, plēbeī or **plēbs, plēbis,** f. plebs, common people

Line 3:   **habeō, habēre, habuī, habitum** to have, hold; *habeō* often means "have" but sometimes, as here, the verb means "hold, consider."

            locus, -ī, m. rank, position; *locus* often occurs in the ablative without the preposition *in* to express place where.

            audeō, audēre, ausus sum to dare; be careful to distinguish between the forms of *audiō, audīre, audīvī, audītum* "to hear" and *audeō, audēre, ausus sum* "to dare."

            adhibeō, adhibēre, adhibuī, adhibitum (+ *dat.*) to invite, summon; note *nūllō* = the dative *nūllī* here.

            consilium, -(i)ī, n. council, deliberation, decision, planning

plērīque, plērōrumque, m. pl. the majority, most people

cum, *conj.* translate "whenever." Usually the conjunction *cum* means "when, since, although," but in some sentences when a general condition is being expressed, *cum* means "whenever."

aes aliēnum, aeris aliēnī, n. debt; *aes aliēnum* means literally "money belonging to another."

tribūtum, -ī, n. tribute, tax

iniūria, -ae, f. wrongdoing, oppression, injury

potēns, potentis powerful; *potentiōrum* is being used as a substantive with the noun *virōrum* understood.

premō, premere, pressī, pressum to suppress, press hard

sēsē: reduplicated form of the reflexive pronoun *sē*

dicō (1) to dedicate, give oneself; be sure to distinguish *dicō* (1), a verb of the first conjugation, from the verb of "saying" *dīcō, dīcere, dīxī, dictum,* which belongs to the third conjugation.

nōbilis, nōbile noble; *nōbilibus* is another substantive with the noun *virīs* understood. Here the word refers to the most distinguished of the Knights (see line 8 below).

quibus and **dominīs:** datives of possession; *eadem ... quae* signify "same ... as." Translate *quibus in hōs eadem omnia sunt iūra quae dominīs in servōs*: "who possess all the same rights toward these as masters [possess] toward slaves."

iūs, iūris, n. right, law, prerogative

alter. . . alter the one . . . the other

druidum . . . equitum genitives of possession; translate *est* as "consists of."

druidēs, druidum, m. pl. Druids

eques, equitis, m. here, knight (Gallic aristocracy)

illī: refers to the Druids because in the previous sentence they had been mentioned first, i.e., *alterum est druidum, alterum equitum.* *Ille* refers to "that one" or the first mentioned (the former), while *hī* refers to "this one" or "these," i.e., the last mentioned (the latter). Note that the Druids are referred to only by pronouns in the rest of this passage.

dīvīnus, -a, -um holy, divine

intersum, interesse, interfuī to take part in, attend to; this compound verb, like many in Latin, governs the dative case.

sacrificium, -ī, n. sacrifice

CAESAR *DĒ BELLŌ GALLICŌ* 6.13, CONTINUED

ac prīvāta prōcūrant, religiōnēs interpretantur: ad hōs magnus
10 adulēscentium numerus disciplīnae causā concurrit, magnōque
hī sunt apud eōs honōre. Nam ferē, dē omnibus contrōversiīs
pūblicīs prīvātīsque cōnstituunt, et, sī quod est admissum facinus,
sī caedēs facta, sī dē hērēditāte, dē fīnibus contrōversia est, īdem
dēcernunt, praemia poenāsque cōnstituunt; sī quī aut prīvātus
15 aut populus eōrum dēcrētō nōn stetit, sacrificiīs interdīcunt.
Haec poena apud eōs est gravissima. Quibus ita est interdictum,
hī numerō impiōrum ac scelerātōrum habentur, hīs omnēs
dēcēdunt, aditum sermōnemque dēfugiunt, nē quid ex contāgiōne
incommodī accipiant, neque hīs petentibus iūs redditur,

NOTES AND VOCABULARY

Line 9:   **prōcūrō** (1) to attend to, administer

religiō, religiōnis, f. religion, religious rites

interpretor, interpretārī, interpretātus sum to interpret, explain

Line 10:   **adulēscēns, adulēscentis,** m./f. young man, young woman, youth

disciplīna, -ae, f. education, knowledge

causā, + *preceding gen.* for the sake of, because of; don't confuse this
use of *causā* with the noun *causa, -ae,* f. "reason."

concurrō, concurrere, concurrī, concursum (+ *ad*) to flock (to) in
crowds, to assemble together

Line 11:   **apud,** *prep. + acc.* among; *apud eōs* = among the Gauls

ferē, *adv.* nearly, almost, usually

contrōversia, -ae, f. dispute

Line 12:   **cōnstituō, cōnstituere, cōnstituī, cōnstitūtum** to decide,
determine, judge

facinus, facinoris, n. crime

Line 13:   **caedēs, caedis,** f. murder

facta: supply *est.*

hērēditās, hērēditātis, f. inheritance

fīnis, fīnis, m. end; pl. boundary

īdem, eadem, idem the same

Line 14:	**dēcernō, dēcernere, dēcrēvī, dēcrētum** to settle, decide
	praemium, -ī, n. reward
	poena, -ae, f. punishment
Line 14–15:	**sī quī ... populus:** translate "if anyone whatever individual or tribe ...."
Line 15:	**dēcrētum, -ī,** n. decision, decree; here, the ablative is used with the intransitive verb *stetit,* which should be translated in the present tense, "abide by."
	sacrificiīs: ablative of separation
	interdīcō, interdīcere, interdīxī, interdictum to banish (someone) from
Line 16:	**Quibus:** dative after *est interdictum.* The pronoun refers to the persons banished. Translate "those who have been banished" (*lit.,* "for those whom it has been banished" or "for those for whom a decree of banishment has been issued").
Line 17:	**impius, -a, -um** impious, wicked
	scelerātus, -a, -um criminal, outlawed
Line 18:	**dēcēdō, dēcēdere, dēcessī, dēcessum** to abandon, leave, withdraw; *hīs* is dative of separation used with a verb compounded with *dē.*
	aditus, aditūs, m. approach, encounter
	sermō, sermōnis, m. talk, conversation
	dēfugiō, dēfugere, dēfūgī to avoid
	nē quid = *nē aliquid*; remember that "after *sī, nisi, num,* or *nē,* all the *ali*'s fall away."
	contāgiō, contāgiōnis, f. contact
Line 19:	**incommodum, -ī,** n. disadvantage, misfortune, harm; *incommodī* is a partitive genitive (genitive of the whole) used with *quid.*
	petō, petere, petīvī, petītum to demand, entreat, seek
	reddō, reddere, reddidī, redditum to give back, restore, render

CAESAR *DĒ BELLŌ GALLICŌ* 6.13, CONTINUED

20 neque honōs ūllus commūnicātur. Hīs autem omnibus druidibus
praeest ūnus, quī summam inter eōs habet auctōritātem. Hōc
mortuō, aut sī quī ex reliquīs excellit dignitāte succēdit, aut, sī
sunt plūrēs parēs, suffrāgiō druidum, nōn numquam etiam armīs
dē prīncipātū contendunt. Hī certō annī tempore in fīnibus
25 Carnūtum, quae regiō tōtīus Galliae media habētur, cōnsīdunt
in locō cōnsecrātō. Hūc omnēs undique quī contrōversiās habent
conveniunt eōrumque dēcrētīs iūdiciīsque parent. Disciplīna in
Britanniā reperta atque inde in Galliam trānslāta esse exīstimātur,
et nunc quī dīligentius eam rem cōgnōscere volunt plērumque illō
30 discendī causā proficīscuntur.

NOTES AND VOCABULARY

Line 20: **commūnicō** (1) to share
Line 21: **praesum, praeesse, praefuī, praefutūrum** to preside over, be in
charge of
summus, -a, -um highest
auctōritās, auctōritātis, f. authority, power, influence
Line 22: **mortuus, -a, -um** dead, deceased
sī quī = *sī aliquī*
reliquus, -a, -um remaining, left over
excellō, excellere, excelluī (+ *abl.*) to excel in, be superior in
dignitās, dignitātis, f. worth, reputation, authority
succēdō, succēdere, successī, successum to advance, become the
successor
Line 23: **plūs, plūris** more, several
pār, paris equal; distinguish carefully between this adjective and the
noun *pars, partis,* f. "part."
suffrāgium, -(i)ī, n. vote; *suffrāgiō* is an ablative of means; take with
contendunt.
numquam, *adv.* never; translate *nōn numquam* "sometimes."
Line 24: **prīncipātus, prīncipātūs,** m. leadership, rule, first place
contendō, contendere, contendī, contentum to fight, compete

Carnūtes, Carnūtum, m. pl. a people in Gaul on both sides of the Loire

regiō, regiōnis, f. region, area

medius, -a, -um middle

cōnsīdō, cōnsīdere, cōnsēdī, cōnsessum to hold sessions, encamp, settle

Line 26: **cōnsecrō** (1) to consecrate, dedicate to the gods

hūc, *adv.* here, to this place

Line 27: **iūdicium, -(i)ī,** n. trial, decision

pareō, parēre, paruī (+ *dat.*) to obey; be careful to distinguish between *parō* (1) "to prepare" and *pareō, parēre, paruī* "to obey." Don't confuse forms of the noun *pars, partis,* f. "part" or the adjective *pār, paris* "equal" with either of these verbs.

disciplīna, -ae, f. system, discipline, knowledge

Line 28: **reperiō, reperīre, repperī, repertum** to find, discover

inde, *adv.* from there

trānsferō, trānsferre, trānstulī, trānslātum to carry across, transfer

exīstimō (1) to consider, think, judge

Line 29: **dīligēns, dīligentis** careful, strict

cōgnōscō, cōgnōscere, cōgnōvī, cōgnitum to know, learn

illō: to that place

Line 30: **discō, discere, didicī** to learn, know

COMPREHENSION QUESTIONS

1. In Gaul, to what group are the plebs considered equivalent? Cite the Latin.

2. Name the two types of men who are respected. Cite the Latin.

3. What are the Druids' chief responsibilities?

4. What happens if people do not abide by their decisions?

5. What possible scenarios may occur when the chief Druid dies? Cite the Latin.

6. Where did the practice of having Druids as arbitrators possibly originate?

READING 2

In 6.14 Caesar provides more information about the Druids, such as they are exempt from military service, they do not entrust their doctrine to writing, and they believe in transmigration of the souls; in 6.15 he discusses the Knights, who are very bellicose; in 6.16 he reveals how some of the Gauls engage in human sacrifice and the role the Druids play in these religious observances.

PRACTICE AND BELIEFS OF THE DRUIDS [14]; THE KNIGHTS [15]; AND HUMAN SACRIFICE [16]

CAESAR *DĒ BELLŌ GALLICŌ* 6.14–16

1   [14] Druidēs ā bellō abesse cōnsuērunt, neque tribūta ūnā cum
    reliquīs pendunt; militiae vacātiōnem omniumque rērum habent
    immunitātem. Tantīs excitātī praemiīs et suā sponte multī in
    disciplīnam conveniunt et ā parentibus propinquīsque mittuntur.

5   Magnum ibi numerum versuum ēdiscere dīcuntur. Itaque annōs
    nōn nūllī XX in disciplīnā permanent. Neque fās esse exīstimant
    ea litterīs mandāre, cum in reliquīs ferē rēbus, pūblicīs prīvātīsque
    ratiōnibus, Graecīs litterīs ūtantur. Id mihi duābus dē causīs
    īnstituisse videntur, quod neque in vulgum disciplīnam efferrī velint

10 neque eōs quī discunt litterīs cōnfīsōs minus memoriae studēre;

NOTES AND VOCABULARY

Line 1:   **ā bellō:** ablative of separation

absum, abesse, afuī, afutūrum to refrain, be absent from

cōnsuescō, cōnsuescere, cōnsuēvī, cōnsuētum to become
accustomed to; *consuērunt* is the contracted form of *cōnsuēvērunt*.

tribūtum, -ī, n. tribute, tax

ūnā, *adv.* together; don't confuse the adverb *ūnā* that means "together"
with the number for "one," *ūnus, -a, -um*.

Line 2:   **pendō, pendere, pependī, pēnsum** to pay

mīlitia, -ae, f. the military, military service

vacātiō, vacātiōnis, f. exemption

Line 3: **immūnitās, immūnitātis,** f. immunity, exception

excitō (1) to rouse, inspire

sponte, f. (*abl. only*) of one's own accord

Line 4: **propinquus, -ī,** m. relative, relation

Line 5: **versus, versūs,** m. verse, line (of poetry)

ēdiscō, ēdiscere, ēdidicī to learn thoroughly or by heart

Line 6: **nōn nūllī:** translate "some"; an example of LITOTES.

permaneō, permanēre, permansī, permānsum to remain

fās, n. *indecl.* right, divine law

exīstimō (1) to consider, judge, think

Line 7: **ea:** translate "these things" or "these principles."

littera, -ae, f. letter (of the alphabet); pl. writing

mandō (1) to entrust, commit

cum, *conj.* when, since, although; use the concessive translation "although."

ferē, *adv.* nearly, almost, usually

Line 8: **ratiō, ratiōnis,** f. account, transaction, business; *ratiōnibus* refers to accounts and general records

ūtor, ūtī, ūsus sum (+ *abl.*) to use

mihi: notice the use of the first person pronoun *mihi.* Caesar's reference to himself in the first person in *dē bellō Gallicō* is very rare.

causa, -ae, f. reason; be careful to distinguish between the look-alike words: *causa, -ae,* f. "reason," *casa, -ae,* f. "hut, house," and *cāsus, cāsūs,* m. "misfortune."

Line 9: **īnstituō, īnstituere, īnstituī, īnstitūtum** to set up, establish

vulgus, -ī, n. crowd, public; *in vulgum* to the general public, publicly

disciplīna, -ae, f. doctrine

Line 10: **discō, discere, didicī** to learn, know

cōnfīdō, cōnfīdere, cōnfīsus sum (+ *dat.*) to rely on, trust; translate *litterīs cōnfīsōs* "relying on writing."

studeō, studēre, studuī (+ *dat.*) to study, apply oneself to

CAESAR *DĒ BELLŌ GALLICŌ* 6.14–16, CONTINUED

quod ferē plērīsque accidit ut praesidiō litterārum dīligentiam
in perdiscendō ac memoriam remittant. In prīmīs hoc volunt
persuādēre, nōn interīre animās sed ab aliīs post mortem trānsīre
ad aliōs, atque hōc maximē ad virtūtem excitārī putant, metū
15 mortis neglēctō. Multa praetereā dē sīderibus atque eōrum mōtū,
dē mundī ac terrārum magnitūdine, dē rērum nātūrā, dē deōrum
immortālium vī ac potestāte disputant et iūventūtī trādunt. [15]
Alterum genus est equitum. Hī, cum est ūsus atque aliquod bellum
incidit (quod ferē ante Caesaris adventum quotannīs accidere
20 solēbat, utī aut ipsī iniūriās īnferrent aut inlātās prōpulsārent),

NOTES AND VOCABULARY

Line 11:   **ferē,** *adv.* almost, generally, for the most part

plērīque, plērōrumque, m. pl. the majority, most people

accidō, accidere, accidī to occur, happen to (+ *dat. of person affected*)

praesidium, -(i)ī, n. help, assistance, protection

Line 12:   **perdiscō, perdiscere, perdidicī** to learn thoroughly, learn by heart;
the prefix of *perdiscendō*, like that of *ēdiscere*, shows that this material
must be overlearned to the point of being part of the person.

remittō, remittere, remīsī, remissum to relax, loosen, release

in prīmīs: among the first, especially

hoc: refers to what follows.

Line 13:   **persuādeō, persuādēre, persuāsī, persuāsum** (+ *dat.*) to convince,
persuade

intereō, interīre, interiī/interivī, interitum to die

Line 13–14:   **ab aliīs ... ad aliōs:** from one ... to another

Line 14:   **hōc:** ablative of means; "by this." The pronoun here refers to what has
just been said.

maximē, *adv.* especially

virtūs, virtūtis, f. excellence, virtue

excitō (1) to rouse, inspire; understand *hominēs* as the subject of
excitārī.

putō (1) to think

metus, metūs, m. fear

Line 15:	**neglegō, neglegere, neglēxī, neglēctum** to disregard
	praetereā, *adv.* besides, moreover
	sīdus, sīderis, n. star, constellation
	mōtus, mōtūs, m. motion, movement
Line 16:	**mundus, -ī,** m. world, universe
Line 17:	**vīs, vīs,** f. force, power, strength
	potestās, potestātis, f. power, authority
	disputō (1) to dispute, discuss, argue
	iuventūs, iuventūtis, f. youth, young people
	trādō, trādere, trādidī, trāditum to pass on, hand down, teach
Line 18:	**eques, equitis,** m. knight; *equitum* is a genitive of possession; note that the opening sentence of 15.1 picks up from 13.1: *eōrum hominum . . . genera sunt duo.*
	usus, usūs, m. use, need
Line 19:	**incidō, incidere, incidī, incasum** to fall in, happen, occur; be careful not to confuse *incidō, incidere, incidī, incasum* "to happen" with *incīdō, incīdere, incīdī, incīsum* "to cut into, cut short." The fourth principal part *incasum* shows that this verb is a compound of *cadō* "to fall, happen," while the verb with the fourth part *incīsum* is from *caedō* "to cut, kill."
	adventus, adventŭs, m. approach, arrival
	quotannīs, *adv.* annually, every year
Line 20:	**soleō, solēre, solitus sum** to be used to, be accustomed to
	ut, utī, *conj.* so that, that, as, when; don't confuse this word with the second principal part of *utor, utī, usus sum* "to use."
	īnferō, īnferre, intulī, illātum to bring forward, inflict
	prōpulsō (1) to drive off, repel

omnēs in bellō versantur; atque eōrum ut quisque est genere
copiīsque amplissimus, ita plūrimōs circum sē ambactōs
clientēsque habet. Hanc ūnam grātiam potentiamque novērunt.
[16] Nātiō est omnis Gallōrum admodum dēdita religiōnibus,

25 atque ob eam causam quī sunt adfectī graviōribus morbīs quīque
in proeliīs perīculīsque versantur aut prō victimīs hominēs
immolant aut sē immolātūrōs vovent, administrīsque ad ea
sacrificia druidibus ūtuntur; quod, prō vītā hominis nisi hominis
vīta reddātur, nōn posse deōrum immortālium nūmen plācārī

30 arbitrantur, pūblicēque ēiusdem generis habent īnstitūta sacrificia.
Aliī immānī magnitūdine simulācra habent, quōrum contexta
vīminibus membra vīvīs hominibus complent; quibus succēnsīs
circumventī flammā exanimantur hominēs. Supplicia eōrum quī in
fūrtō aut in latrōciniō aut aliquā noxiā sint comprehēnsī grātiōra

NOTES AND VOCABULARY

Line 21:   **versor** (1) to occupy oneself with, be engaged in
            quisque, quidque, *pron.* each, each one, everybody
            genere: "in terms of birth"

Lines 21–22: **ut quisque** + superlative **... ita:** translate "the more each ... so the
            more."

Line 22:   **amplus, -a, -um** powerful, strong, prominent
            plūrimus, -a, -um most, very great, very many
            ambactus, -ī, m. vassal

Line 23:   **ūnam:** translate "only."
            grātia, -ae, f. influence, favor
            potentia, -ae, f. force, power
            nōscō, nōscere, nōvī, nōtum to learn, recognize; in perfect tenses,
            to know

Line 24:   **nātiō, nātiōnis,** f. nation, race, people
            admodum, *adv.* very, quite, just about
            dēdō, dēdere, dēdidī, dēditum to devote, give up

religiō, religiōnis, f. piety to the gods; (pl.) religious observances, religious matters

Line 25: **adficiō, adficere, adfēcī, adfectum** to affect, impair

gravis, grave serious, severe

morbus, -ī, m. sickness, disease

Line 26: **proelium, -(i)ī,** n. battle, fight

Line 27: **immolō** (1) to sacrifice

voveō, vovēre, vōvī, vōtum to pledge, devote

administer, administrī, m. assistant

Line 28: **nisi,** *conj.* unless, if not, except

Line 29: **nūmen, nūminis,** n. divine will, divine power, divinity

plācō (1) to calm, appease

Line 30: **arbitror** (1) to consider, judge, think; note that *arbitror* is a synonym of *putō* and *existimō*, both appearing in these passages written by Caesar.

pūblicē, *adv.* on behalf of the state, as a community, publicly

īnstituō, īnstituere, īnstituī, īnstitūtum to put in place, establish, build; translate *habent īnstitūta sacrificia* "have sacrifices established."

Line 31: **immānis, immāne** huge, enormous

simulācrum, -ī, n. likeness, image, representation

contexō, contexere, contexuī, contextum to weave together, entwine

Line 32: **vīmen, vīminis,** n. twig, basket

membrum, -ī, n. limb, part

compleō, complēre, complēvī, complētum to fill, complete; *aliī* is the subject

succendō, succendere, succendī, succēnsum to set fire to, light

Line 33: **circumveniō, circumvenīre, circumvēnī, circumventum** to enclose, surround

exanimō (1) to kill

supplicium, -ī, n. supplication, punishment, execution

Line 34: **fūrtum, -ī,** n. theft, trick

latrōcinium, -ī, n. robbery, banditry

noxia, -ae, f. harm, crime

comprehendō, comprehendere, comprehendī, comprehēnsum to capture, arrest

CAESAR *DĒ BELLŌ GALLICŌ* 6.14–16, CONTINUED

35   dīs immortalibus esse arbitrantur, sed, cum ēius generis cōpia

      dēficit, etiam ad innocentium supplicia dēscendunt.

NOTES AND VOCABULARY

Line 35:   **deus, -ī,** m. god; *dīs* is the irregular dative/ablative plural.

Line 36:   **dēficiō, dēficere, dēfēcī, dēfectum** to fail, run out

           innocēns, innocentis innocent, blameless

           dēscendō, dēscendere, dēscendī, dēscēnsum to fall, stoop, resort to, lower oneself

COMPREHENSION QUESTIONS

1. What is not required of the Druids, unlike others?

2. Why do they not entrust information to writing?

3. How does Caesar characterize the Knights?

4. Why do the Gauls engage in human sacrifice?

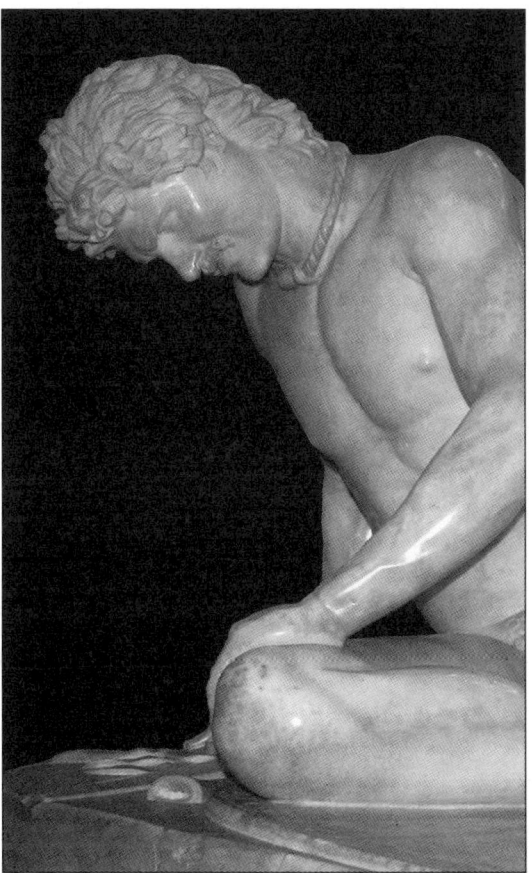

The Dying Gaul. Marble replica of one of the sculptures in the ex-voto group dedicated to Pergamon by Attalus I to commemorate the victories over the Galatians in the 3rd and 2nd centuries BCE. A detail of this statue is on the cover. Capitoline Museums, Rome. (© Wikimedia Commons)

READING 3

In Book 3 of the *Civil War*, Caesar describes how Pompey fled to Egypt after the battle of Pharsalus and how he is killed by one of King Ptolemy's men and by a former supporter who served with him in the war against the pirates.

POMPEY ASKS KING PTOLEMY FOR ASYLUM

CAESAR *DĒ BELLŌ CĪVĪLĪ* 103

1   103. Ibi cāsū rēx erat Ptolemaeus, puer aetāte, magnīs cōpiīs cum sorōre Cleopatrā bellum gerēns, quam paucīs ante mēnsibus per suōs propinquōs atque amīcōs rēgnō expulerat; castraque Cleopatrae nōn longō spatiō ab ēius castrīs distābant. Ad eum Pompēius

5   mīsit, ut prō hospitiō atque amīcitiā patris Alexandrīā reciperētur atque illīus opibus in calamitāte tegerētur. Sed quī ab eō missī erant, cōnfectō lēgātiōnis officiō, līberius cum mīlitibus rēgis conloquī coepērunt eōsque hortārī ut suum officium Pompēiō praestārent nēve ēius fortūnam dēspicerent. In hōc erant

NOTES AND VOCABULARY

Line 1:   **ibi,** *adv.* at that time

cāsus, cāsūs, m. chance; distinguish carefully between this fourth declension noun and the first declension noun *casa, -ae,* f. "hut, house."

Ptolemaeus, -ī, m. Ptolemy

aetas, aetātis, f. age; *aetāte* is an ablative of respect. At that time Ptolemy was around 13 years of age.

Line 2:   **Cleopatra, -ae,** f. Cleopatra; at that time Cleopatra was around 19 years of age.

quam: the relative pronoun refers to Cleopatra.

mēnsis, mēnsis, m. month; translate *paucīs ante mēnsibus,* which is an ablative of degree of difference, "a few months earlier"; literally "before by a few months."

Line 3:	**propinquus, -ī,** m. relative
	rēgnum, -ī, n. kingdom; *rēgnō* is an ablative of separation.
	expellō, expellere, expulī, expulsum to drive out, expel
	castra, -ōrum, n. (military) camp; note plural form with singular meaning.
Line 4:	**spatium, -(i)ī,** n. distance; *longō spatiō* is an ablative of degree of difference with *distābant.*
	ēius: refers to Ptolemy.
	distō (1) to stand apart
	Pompēius, Pompēī, m. Pompey (the Great)
Line 5:	**mittō, mittere, mīsī, missum** to send a request; the *ut* clause is in apposition to the notion of request implied in the verb.
	prō (*prep.* + *abl.*) by virtue of, in return for
	hospitium, -(i)ī, n. hospitality, guest-host relationship
	patris: King Ptolmey's father; Ptolemy XII Auletes stayed with Pompey when he was in exile in the 50's BCE.
	Alexandrīā: ablative used instead of the locative for place where.
	recipiō, recipere, recēpī, receptum to receive
Line 6:	**illīus:** refers to Ptolemy
	opēs, opium, f. power, resources
	calamitās, calamitātis, f. misfortune
	tegō, tegere, tēxī, tēctum to protect
	quī: translate "those who."
	ab eō: refers to Pompey
Line 7:	**conficiō, conficere, confēcī, confectum** to complete
	lēgātiō, lēgātiōnis, f. embassy, mission
	officium, -ī, n. duty
	līberius, *comparative adv.* too freely
Line 8:	**conloquor, conloquī, conlocūtus sum** to speak with
	coepī, coepisse to begin (defective verb)
	hortor (1) to urge
Lines 8–9:	**suum officium praestāre:** translate "that they discharge their duty."
Line 9:	**nēve,** *adv.* and not
	dēspiciō, dēspicere, dēspexī, dēspectum to look down on

CAESAR *DĒ BELLŌ CĪVĪLĪ* 103, CONTINUED

10   numerō complūrēs Pompēī mīlitēs, quōs ex ēius exercitū acceptōs
     in Syriā Gabīnius Alexandrīam trādūxerat bellōque cōnfectō apud
     Ptolemaeum, patrem puerī, relīquerat.

NOTES AND VOCABULARY

Line 10: **complūrēs, complūrium** several
          ēius: refers to Pompey

Line 11: **in Syriā:** After Pompey's campaign in Syria, some of his troops were
          left behind there to defend the recently annexed territory.

          Gabīnius, -ī, m. Aulus Gabinius, now one of Caesar's officers;
          although previously Gabinius had been a strong supporter of
          Pompey and had served as one of his officers, during the Civil Wars
          he supported Caesar.

          trādūcō, trādūcere, trādūxī, trāductum to lead across

          apud, *prep. + acc.* with, in the presence of

Line 12: **relinquō, relinquere, relīquī, relictum** to leave behind

COMPREHENSION QUESTIONS

1. What age was King Ptolemy at this time? Cite the Latin.

2. Who helped King Ptolemy drive Cleopatra out of his kingdom?

3. What request did Pompey make of King Ptolemy?

4. Whom did Gabinius bring to Alexandria? Cite the Latin.

Sphinx and Pompey's Pillar in Alexandria, Egypt. Medieval travelers to Egypt believed that Pompey must have been buried here and that the capital of the red Aswan granite column contained his head. Thus this pillar was named Pompey's pillar when in fact the pillar was built in the 4th century in honor of the Emperor Diocletian who had captured Alexandria. (© 2013 Shutterstock Images LLC)

READING 4

Key advisers to Ptolemy decide to kill Pompey. Lucius Septimius, who formerly had served in one of Pompey's campaigns, assists with executing the murder.

THE DEATH OF POMPEY

CAESAR *DĒ BELLŌ CĪVĪLĪ* 104

1   104. Hīs tunc cōgnitīs rēbus, amīcī rēgis, quī propter aetātem
    ēius in cūrātiōne erant rēgnī, sīve timōre adductī, ut posteā
    praedicābant, sollicitātō exercitū regiō, nē Pompēius Alexandrīam
    Aegyptumque occupāret, sīve dēspectā ēius fortūnā, ut

5   plērumque in calamitāte ex amīcīs inimīcī exsistunt, hīs quī
    erant eō missī palam respondērunt eumque ad rēgem venīre
    iussērunt; ipsī, clam cōnsiliō initō, Achillam, praefectum rēgium,
    singulārī hominem audāciā, et L. Septimium, tribūnum mīlitum,
    ad interficiendum Pompēium mīsērunt. Ab hīs līberāliter ipse

10 appellātus et quādam nōtitiā Septimī prōductus, quod bellō
    praedōnum apud eum ōrdinem dūxerat, nāviculam parvulam

NOTES AND VOCABULARY

Line 1:   **cōgnōscō, cōgnōscere, cōgnōvī, cōgnitum** to learn; in perfect
            tenses, to know

            amīcī rēgis: these included Achillas, army commander or prefect,
            mentioned in line 7; Pothinus, royal guardian; and Theodotus of
            Chios, the young king's tutor

Line 2:   **ēius:** refers to Ptolemy

            in cūrātiōne erant rēgnī: translate "were acting as regents"; literally:
            "were in the administration of the kingdom."

            sīve ... sīve, *conj.* whether ... or

            addūcō, addūcere, addūxī, adductum to influence

            posteā, *adv.* afterwards

Line 3:   **praedicō** (1) to allege

sollicitō (1) to offer bribes to, stir up

sollicitātō exercitū regiō: either supply "by Pompey" with this ablative absolute or construe the ablative absolute as part of the *nē* clause that follows.

regiō, regiōnis, f. region; be careful not to confuse the many Latin words that begin with *reg-* such as *rēx, rēgis,* m. "king" (cf. line 1); *rēgnum, -ī,* n. "kingdom" (cf. line 2); *rēgnō* (1) "to rule"; *regō* "to rule, guide"; *rēgius, -a, -um* "royal"; and from this line *regiō* "region."

Line 5:   **plērumque,** *adv.* very often

exsistō, existere, exsistī to prove to be, show oneself

hīs: indirect object of *respondērunt,* one of the two main verbs of this sentence

Line 6:   **eō,** *adv.* there; be careful not to confuse this adverb with the ablative singular masculine and neuter forms of *is, ea, id.*

palam, *adv.* in the open, in public

Line 7:   **clam,** *adv.* secretly (in contrast to *palam* in line 5)

inīre cōnsilium: to form a plan

Line 8:   **singulāris, singulāre** remarkable, extraordinary

singulārī . . . audāciā: ablative of description

L. Septimius: Lūcius Septimius, a Roman officer who had served in Pompey's campaign against the pirates

Line 9:   **hīs:** refers to Achillas and Septimius

līberāliter, *adv.* generously, kindly

ipse: refers to Pompey

Line 10:   **quīdam, quaedam, quoddam,** *indefinite pron.* and *adj.,* certain, a certain

nōtitia, -ae, f. acquaintance

prōdūcō, prōdūcere, prōdūxī, prōductum to induce

Line 11:   **praedō, praedōnis,** m. pirate

ōrdinem dūxerat: translate "had commanded a division."

nāvicula, -ae, f. small vessel, skiff; note how the double diminutive, *nāviculam parvulam,* adds poignancy to the passage.

CAESAR *DĒ BELLŌ CĪVĪLĪ* 104, CONTINUED

cōnscendit cum paucīs suīs; ibi ab Achillā et Septimiō interficitur.
Item L. Lentulus comprehenditur ab rēge et in custōdiā necātur.

NOTES AND VOCABULARY

Line 12:   **cōnscendō, cōnscendere, cōnscendī, cōnscēnsum** to board, go on
board

paucīs suīs: *paucī* is being used as a substantive here. Understand *virīs*
or *mīlitibus*.

Line 13:   **L. (Lucius) Lentulus:** consul in 49 BCE and one of Pompey's strongest
supporters

comprehendō, comprehendere, comprehēndī, comprehēnsum to
seize

necō (1) to kill

COMPREHENSION QUESTIONS

1. Who replied to Pompey's request?

2. What was their response? Cite the Latin.

3. What did they later say caused them to make this response?

4. Whom did they send to kill Pompey?

5. Why did Pompey trust Septimius enough to board the boat? Cite
the Latin.

CHAPTER 2

GAIUS VALERIUS CATULLUS

AN INTRODUCTION TO CATULLUS

Gaius Valerius Catullus is one of Rome's most beloved and influential poets. The time during which he lived, however, was tumultuous, characterized by the aftermath of Sulla's dictatorship (82–79 BCE), by the slave revolt of Spartacus (73–71 BCE), by the conspiracy of Catiline to overthrow the state (63 BCE), and by the jockeying for power by three ambitious and ruthless men, Marcus Crassus, Julius Caesar, and Gnaeus Pompey, in the years 70 BCE and following.

Catullus was born in Verona, Italy to a wealthy and prominent family, around 84 BCE, and died in Rome some thirty years later, around 54–52 BCE. Catullus was sent to Rome to receive an education that would lead to a career in law and/or politics. From his poetry we learn that Catullus served on the staff of the praetorian governor Gaius Memmius who was assigned the province of Bithynia (57–56 BCE).

Catullus wrote poems on many topics, including love, friendship, poetry, marriage, his and his friends' experiences in the provinces, and social mores. His poems also contain sometimes bitter attacks on rivals. But he is most well known for the series of love poems about a woman whom he refers to as "Lesbia." Most critics believe that the Lesbia poems are based on a real-life experience. The name Lesbia alludes to the Greek lyric poetess Sappho of Lesbos, whose love poetry influenced Catullus. Almost certainly "Lesbia" is a pseudonym for the very aristocratic Clodia, wife of Quintus Caecilius Metellus Celer and the older sister of the notorious Publius Clodius Pulcher. The love affair proved to be tempestuous because Catullus the lover expected fidelity from his lady while Lesbia's/

Clodia's apparently flirtatious character attracted the attention of a number of admirers. One of these admirers was Marcus Caelius Rufus, who betrayed his friend Catullus by becoming involved with Lesbia/Clodia.

Cicero called Catullus and like-minded poets of his generation "the new poets" or neoterics (*poetae novi* or *neoteri*), who discovered in Alexandrian literature of the third century literary values that were relevant and adaptable to their own literary ideals. Like their Alexandrian predecessors, these poets were interested in experimenting with meter, language, content, style, and genre. They preferred short poems over long, discursive epics, and personal poetry over that concerned with the public sphere. They embraced the qualities of originality, erudition, and refinement.

Catullus's poetry is lively and entertaining, and the characters he introduces are unforgettable. The topics of love and friendship transcend time; the poetry seems as relevant and timely today as when Catullus composed it over two thousand years ago.

Monument of Memmius. Erected in the time of Augustus, this monument in Ephesus shows Gaius Memmius and Sulla, his father-in-law. Gaius Memmius's career demonstrates how interconnected the worlds of military service, politics, and literature were at this time. Catullus served under Memmius when he was the governor of Bithynia. Memmius divorced Sulla's daughter Fausta in 55, stood for consul with Caesar's support in 54, was condemned for *abitus* (obtaining electoral support through gifts), and went into exile in 52 BCE. In addition to his relationship to the poet Catullus, Memmius was the dedicatee of the poet Lucretius's *De Rerum Natura*. (© 2013 Shutterstock Images LLC)

READING 5

Poem 11 forms the culmination of an opening sequence of love poems that succinctly tell the story of Catullus's love affair with Lesbia. The sequence moves from the beginnings of love in Poems 2 and 3 to the height of passion in the kissing Poems 5 and 7 and then to disillusionment in Poem 8 and to renunciation in Poem 11. In Poem 8 Catullus the lover cannot bring himself to refer to Lesbia by name. In Poem 11 he cannot bear the thought of facing his girl himself with his message of dismissal, and so sends Furius and Aurelius as intermediaries to tell her that the love affair is over. There is a hint of humor when it is revealed midway through the poem that the dangerous mission Catullus has in mind for his companions is to deliver a message from him to Lesbia.

FAREWELL TO LESBIA

CATULLUS *CARMEN* 11

Meter: Sapphic stanza

1   Fūrī et Aurēlī, comitēs Catullī,
    sīve in extrēmōs penetrābit Indōs,
    lītus ut longē resonante Eōā
        tunditur undā,
5   sīve in Hyrcanōs Arabāsve mollēs,
    seu Sagās sagittiferōsve Parthōs,
    sīve quae septemgeminus colōrat
        aequora Nīlus,

NOTES AND VOCABULARY

Line 1:   Furius and Aurelius appear in other poems in the collection. Many
           believe that Furius and Aurelius are not truly Catullus's friends, but
           are ironically addressed as such in this poem. Catullus imagines
           Furius and Aurelius accompanying him on campaigns, first in the
           East (lines 1–8), then in the West (lines 9–12).

   comes, comitis, m. companion, comrade (*lit.* "one who goes with"); in
   apposition to *Furī* and *Aurēlī.*

Line 2:	**sīve,** *conj.* whether ... or
	extrēmus, -a, -um furthest
	penetrō (1) to make one's way to; Catullus is the subject of the verb.
	Indī, Indōrum, m. pl. the inhabitants of India; translate as "India."
Line 3:	**lītus, lītoris,** n. shore; *lītus* belongs in the *ut* clause and is the subject of *tunditur.*
	longē, *adv.* far, far and wide; modifies *resonante.*
	ut: where (a rare meaning)
	resonō (1) to resound, echo
	Eōus, -a, -um eastern (*lit.* of Eos, goddess of the dawn)
Line 4:	**tundō, tundere, tutudī, tūnsum** to buffet, to beat repeatedly; sound complements meaning in these two lines, with the *und-* element of *unda* echoing *tunditur* (ASSONANCE).
Line 5:	**Hyrcanī, -ōrum,** m. pl. people living on the shores of the Caspian Sea; translate as "Hyrcania."
	Arabs, Arabis, m. Arab; adjective used as a substantive.
	-ve, *conj.* or
	mollis, molle effeminate, soft; *Arabās mollēs,* so described because of their wealth and luxurious way of life.
Line 6:	The preposition *in* should be supplied in lines 6 and 7.
	Sagae, -ārum, m. pl. Scythians; translate as "Scythia."
	sagittifer, sagittifera, sagittiferum arrow-bearing, carrying arrows; the *sag-* element in *sagittifer* repeats the initial syllable of the word for "Scythians," *Sagae.*
	Parthī, -ōrum, m. pl. Parthians; people living in Parthia, a land northeast of Syria, bounded by the Tigris and Euphrates rivers. This is modern-day Iraq.
Line 7:	**quae:** a relative pronoun that refers to *aequora* and serves as the object of *colōrat.*
	septemgeminus, -a, -um sevenfold (*lit.*); here, having seven mouths
	colōrō (1) color, stain (i.e., with the Nile's muddy waters)
Line 8:	**aequor, aequoris,** n. plain, delta, sea (*aequor* refers to any smooth or level surface; the meaning of the word here is ambiguous and may refer to either the delta or the Mediterranean sea.)
	Nīlus, -ī, m. Nile river

CATULLUS *CARMEN* 11, CONTINUED

> sīve trāns altās gradiētur Alpēs,
>
> 10   Caesaris vīsēns monimenta magnī,
>
> Gallicum Rhēnum, horribile aequor ulti-
>
>   mōsque Britannōs,
>
> omnia haec, quaecumque feret voluntās
>
> caelitum, temptāre simul parātī,
>
> 15   pauca nuntiāte meae puellae
>
>   nōn bona dicta.
>
> cum suīs vīvat valeatque moechīs,
>
> quōs simul complexa tenet trecentōs,
>
> nūllum amāns vērē, sed identidem omnium
>
> 20   īlia rumpēns;
>
> nec meum respectet, ut ante, amōrem,

NOTES AND VOCABULARY

Line 9:   **gradior, gradī, gressus sum** to go, journey

            Alpēs, Alpium, f. pl. Alps

Line 10:   **vīsō, visēre, vīsī** to go and see

            monimentum, -ī, n. trophy, testimonial, monument; the places that follow in apposition to *monimentum* serve to remind the reader of the deeds of great Caesar that took place in 55 BCE: his brief excursion from Gaul into Germany by building a temporary bridge across the Rhine and his crossing the English Channel to make his way to Britain; *magnus* here may be ironic.

Line 11:   **Gallicus, -a, -um** of Gaul

            Rhēnus, -ī, m. the Rhine, a river that separates Gaul from Germany

            horribile aequor: "the rough sea" refers to the English Channel; the elided *Rhēnum horribile aequor*, combined with the ASYNDETON, accelerates the conclusion of the travelogue. *Ulti-mōsque* in line 11; *omnium* in line 19, which elides with *īlia* in line 20; and *prātī* in line 22, which elides with *ultimī* in line 23, are examples of hypermetry. This term refers to hyphenation or the elision of a closing syllable at the end of the line with the syllable that opens the next line of poetry.

Line 13:	**omnia haec:** object of *temptāre* in line 14; the phrase refers to the catalogue of places in the preceding lines.
	quīcumque, quaecumque, quodcumque whatever
	voluntās, voluntātis, f. wish, will
Line 14:	**caeles, caelitis,** m./f. heaven-dweller, god; *caelitum* is genitive plural.
	temptō (1) to try
	simul, *adv.* together, at the same time
Line 15:	**nuntiō** (1) to announce, speak
Line 16:	**dictum, dictī,** n. word
	nōn bona dicta: note the LITOTES.
Line 17:	**vīvō, vīvere, vīxī, victum** to live; *vīvat* and *valeat* are volitive subjunctives.
	valeō, valēre, valuī to be strong, be healthy, thrive
	moechus, -ī, m. adulterer
Line 18:	**complector, complectī, complexus sum** to embrace
	trecentī, trecentae, trecenta three hundred; the chiastic word order here, *quōs complexa tenet trecentōs,* suggests that the three hundred adulterers are embracing Lesbia (at the same time that grammatically she is embracing them).
Line 19:	**vērē,** *adv.* truly
	identidem, *adv.* continually, again and again; the many elisions (*identidem* and *omnium,* in addition to the elision of *nūllum* and *amāns*) in this line express intense emotion.
Line 20:	**īlia, īlium,** n. pl., groin, loins
	rumpō, rumpere, rūpī, ruptum to break, burst
Line 21:	**respectō** (1) to look back upon; volitive subjunctive.
	ut, *conj.* as; note the unusual SIMILE in lines 22–24. The flower that more commonly would refer to the love of a woman for a man here refers to the love of a man for a woman; and the plow that would normally refer to the man here refers to a woman.
	ante, *adv.* before

CATULLUS *CARMEN* 11, CONTINUED

> quī illīus culpā cecidit velut prātī
>
> ultimī flōs, praetereunte postquam
>
> > tāctus arātrō est.

NOTES AND VOCABULARY

Line 22: **quī:** a relative pronoun that looks back to *amōrem.*

illīus: this genitive refers to Lesbia; translate "her."

culpa, -ae, f., fault; ablative of cause

cadō, cadere, cecidī, casum to fall, die

velut, *adv.* just as

prātum, -ī, n. meadow

Line 23: **ultimus, -a, -um** at the edge of

flōs, flōris, m. flower

praetereō, praeterīre, praeterīvī, praeteritum to pass, go past

Line 24: **tangō, tangere, tetigī, tāctum** to graze, touch

arātrum, -ī, n. plow

COMPREHENSION QUESTIONS

1. Name at least four places in the East that Catullus imagines Furius and Aurelius visiting. Cite the Latin.

2. What monuments of great Caesar does Catullus imagine Furius and Aurelius will see? Cite the Latin.

3. At the end of their imaginary adventure what does Catullus want Furius and Aurelius to say to Lesbia? Cite the Latin.

4. To what does Catullus compare the love Lesbia has lost?

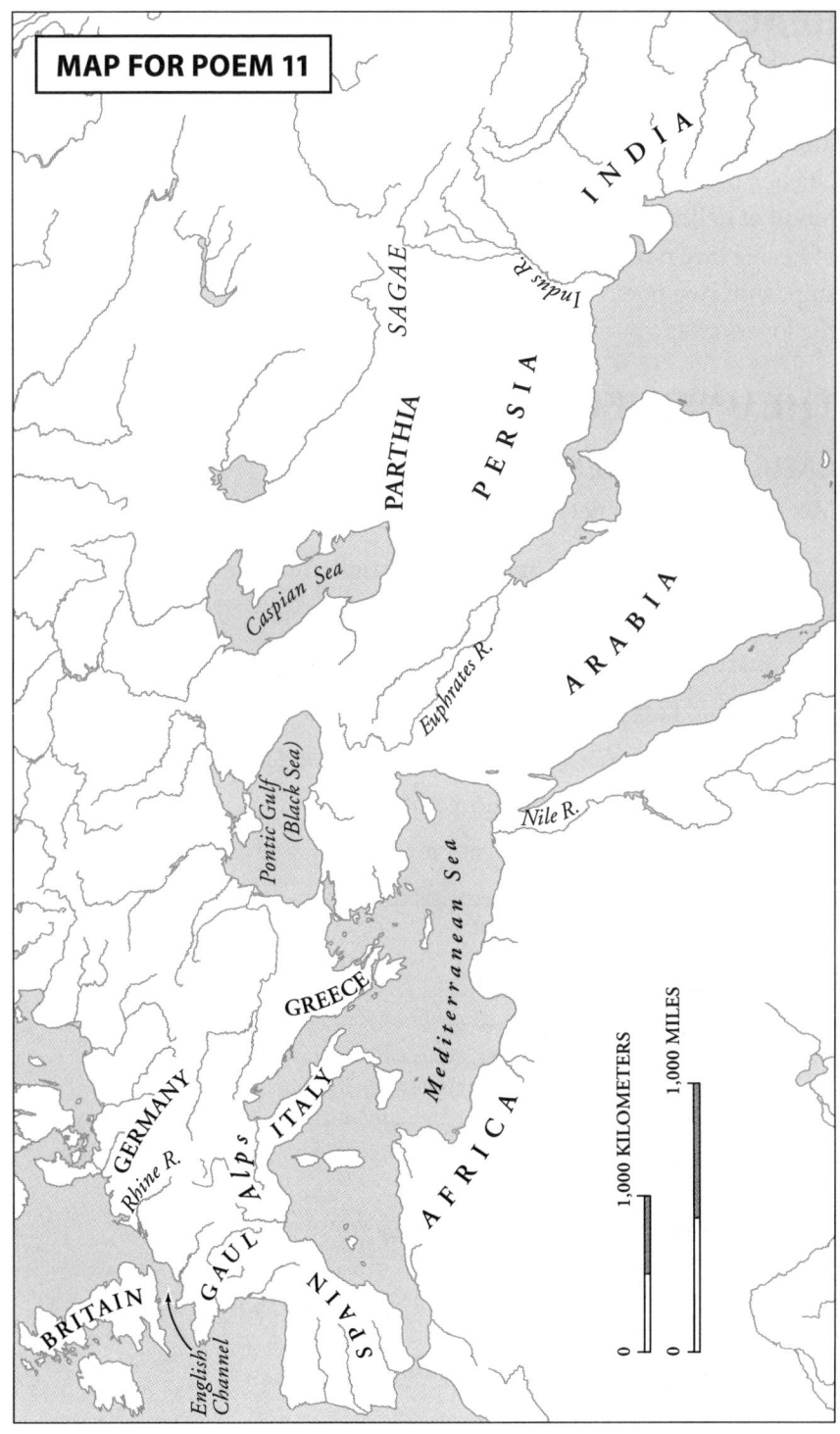

MAP FOR POEM 11

INDIA

SAGAE

PARTHIA

PERSIA

Indus R.

Caspian Sea

ARABIA

Euphrates R.

Pontic Gulf
(Black Sea)

Nile R.

Mediterranean Sea

GREECE

GERMANY

Rhine R.

ITALY

Alps

AFRICA

GAUL

BRITAIN

SPAIN

English
Channel

1,000 KILOMETERS

1,000 MILES

0

0

READING 6

Possibly the most rapturously happy love poem contained in the collection, Poem 107 celebrates the unexpected return of Lesbia to Catullus. The repeated language, which suggests strong emotion, and the many elisions that occur within these eight lines effectively contribute to the mood of delirious joy. It is notable that Catullus chose to end the series of Lesbia love poems, which chronicle their on-again, off-again relationship, with two poems (107 and 109) that deal with the reconciliation of the lovers after a period of estrangement.

THE UNEXPECTED RECONCILIATION

CATULLUS *CARMEN* 107

Meter: Elegiac Couplets

1   Sī quicquam cupidō optantīque optigit umquam
        īnspērantī, hoc est grātum animō propriē.
    quārē hoc est grātum nōbīs quoque, cārius aurō,
        quod tē restituis, Lesbia, mī cupidō.
5   restituis cupidō atque īnspērantī, ipsa refers tē
        nōbīs. ō lūcem candidiōre nōtā!
    quis mē ūnō vīvit fēlīcior, aut magis umquam
        optandam vītam dūcere quis poterit?

NOTES AND VOCABULARY

Line 1:   **quisquam, quicquam,** *pronoun,* anyone, anything

cupidus, -a, -um longing, desirous; one must understand that the missing dative noun that is described by *cupidō, optantī,* and *īnspērantī* is "a person" or "an individual." *cupidō* does not elide with *optantī.* The lack of elision where elision is expected is called hiatus.

optō (1) to desire, wish

optingō, optingere, optigī to happen, occur

umquam, *adv.* ever

Line 2:   **īnspērāns, īnspērantis** not expecting or hoping

grātus, -a, -um pleasing

propriē, *adv.* properly, particularly

Line 3:	**quārē,** *adv.* therefore
	nōbīs: poetic plural for singular
	quoque, *adv.* also, too
	cārus, -a, -um dear
	cārius: this comparative adjective is neuter because it modifies *hoc.*
	aurō: ablative of comparison
Line 4:	**restituō, restituere, restituī, restitūtum** to restore; the repeated language in the poem's center (lines 4–6) nicely conveys the lover's delirious joy at his beloved's unexpected return.
	mī: shortened form of *mihī*
Line 5:	**ipsa:** modifies the understood second singular verb *restituis.*
	referō, referre, rettulī, relātum to bring back, return
	tē: the direct object of both *restituis* and *refers* because both verbs are transitive and thus require an object.
Line 6:	**lūcem:** accusative of exclamation "O day with a whiter mark!" The white mark indicates the day is lucky. Since *lux* can refer to the light of day, by extension, the word comes to mean "day."
	nōta, -ae, f. mark, sign; ablative of description
Lines 7–8:	The text in lines 7 and 8 is corrupt: *aut magis †hac est/†optandus vita dicere.* We follow the emendation of the text suggested by R.O.A.M. Lyne (*Hermes* 118 [1985] 498–500).
Line 7:	**mē ūnō:** ablative of comparison; here *ūnō* means "alone."
	vīvit = *est*
	fēlīx, fēlīcis happy, fortunate, lucky; *fēlīcior* is a comparative adjective.
	magis, *adv.* more; *magis* modifies *optandam.*
Line 8:	**optandam:** a future passive participle that functions as an adjective modifying *vītam.* Translate as "desired."

COMPREHENSION QUESTIONS

1. What is, in Catullus's mind, "dearer than gold"?

2. What is the presumed answer to the questions Catullus raises in lines 7–8?

READING 7

Poem 109 is the last Lesbia love poem in the collection. This poem is surprising because Lesbia here proposes a relationship on Catullus's terms, one that will be based on mutual love and will last forever. Poem 109 is intended to be read closely with Poem 107, with which it shares the theme of reconciliation. The tone of this poem is more subdued, however, suggesting that Catullus has had time to reflect on Lesbia's unexpected return. In light of the tempestuous character of the love affair, it is no wonder that Catullus worries about the sincerity of the proposal.

LESBIA'S PROPOSAL OF EVERLASTING LOVE

CATULLUS *CARMEN* 109

Meter: Elegiac Couplets

1   Iūcundum, mea vīta, mihī prōpōnis amōrem

   hunc nostrum inter nōs perpetuumque fore.

dī magnī, facite ut vērē prōmittere possit,

   atque id sincērē dīcat et ex animō,

5   ut liceat nōbīs tōtā perdūcere vītā

   aeternum hoc sānctae foedus amīcitiae.

NOTES AND VOCABULARY

Line 1:   **iūcundus, -a, -um** pleasant

mea vīta: a term of endearment referring to Lesbia

prōpōnō, prōpōnere, prōposuī, prōpositum to propose, suggest; *prōpōnis* introduces indirect statement, with *amōrem* serving as the subject of the infinitive *fore*.

Line 2:   **noster, nostra, nostrum** of ours, our

fore: contracted from *futūrum esse*, the future infinitive of the verb *sum*.

Line 3:   **facite:** translate "grant"; takes a noun clause introduced by *ut* to express result.

prōmittō, prōmittere, prōmīsī, prōmissum to promise

Line 4:   **sincērē,** *adv.* honestly, sincerely

Line 5:	**ut liceat:** *ut* may be introducing either a result or purpose clause. The impersonal verb *liceat* often takes a dative object.
	tōtā ... vītā: a rare ablative expressing duration of time; note how *vītā* in line 5 recalls *vīta* in line 1.
	perdūcō, perdūcere, perdūxī, perductum to maintain
Line 6:	**foedus, foederis,** n. pact, contract; in lines 5–6 Catullus tries to express the unique quality of the relationship he desires with Lesbia. Catullus wants commitment based on mutual respect and obligation. In other words, Catullus wants a relationship with Lesbia that is equivalent to marriage and at the same time similar to the *amīcitia* that he shares with his male friends.
	sāncta amīcitia: inviolate friendship; note the SYNCHESIS in which *aeternum hoc* describes *foedus* and *sanctae* modifies *amīcitiae*. By employing this figure of speech, Catullus closely connects the thought of an eternal bond and friendship.

COMPREHENSION QUESTIONS

1. What does Catullus say that Lesbia has proposed?

2. In what manner does Catullus hope (in his request to the gods) that Lesbia is making this proposal? Cite the Latin.

3. For how long does Catullus hope that their *foedus amīcitiae* will last? Cite the Latin.

READING 8

Catullus reproaches Rufus for stealing Lesbia from him and for betraying their friendship.

RUFUS'S BETRAYAL

CATULLUS *CARMEN* 77

Meter: Elegiac Couplets

1   Rūfe mihī frustrā ac nēquīquam crēdite amīce
        (frustrā? immō magnō cum pretiō atque malō)
    sīcine subrēpstī mī, atque intestīna perūrens
        ei miserō ēripuistī omnia nostra bona?
5   ēripuistī heu heu nostrae crūdēle venēnum
        vītae, heu heu nostrae pestis amīcitiae.

NOTES AND VOCABULARY

Line 1:   **Rūfe:** vocative of Rufus. Caelius Rufus, protégé of Cicero, was successfully defended by the distinguished orator in the speech on his behalf, the *Prō Caeliō*. Rufus apparently was a friend of Catullus until he became involved with Lesbia.

mihī: dative to be taken either with *amīce* or with *crēdite*. In the latter instance, *mihī* is a dative of agent with a perfect passive participle.

frustrā ac nēquīquam: the two adverbs are synonyms; in vain, to no purpose

crēdō, crēdere, crēdidī, crēditum to believe, suppose

amīcus, -ī, m. friend

Line 2:   **immō,** *adv.* on the contrary, no indeed

pretium, -(i)ī, n. price, cost

malum, -ī, n. misfortune, harm

Line 3:   **sīcine,** *interrogatory adv.* thus, so

subrēps(is)tī: syncopated second person singular perfect from *subrēpō, subrēpere, subrēpsī, subrēptum* to creep up on (someone) unawares, steal upon; the image is that of a snake stealthily stealing upon its victim.

mī: shortened form of *mihī*; dative with the compound verb *subrēpō*.

intestīnum, -ī, n. intestines

perūrō, perūrere, perussī, perustum to burn through and through, consume

ei: monosyllabic interjection expressing distress or anguish. Do not confuse *ei* with the dative singular of *is, ea, id (eī)*, which has a macron over the "i."

miser, misera, miserum unhappy, wretched; understand *mihi* here. The adjective *miserō* is a dative of separation with the verb *ēripiō*.

ēripiō, ēripere, ēripuī, ēreptum to snatch away

omnia nostra bona: this expression alludes to Lesbia.

heu, *interj*. alas; note the ANAPHORA in lines 5–6.

crūdēlis, crūdēle cruel

venēnum, -ī, n. poison

pestis, pestis, m. a deadly disease, plague, bane; note that *nostrae vītae* and *nostrae amīcitiae* are brilliantly ambiguous expressions. The phrase *nostrae vītae* can refer to Catullus, and it can refer also to Lesbia as in Poem 109.1 (*mea vīta*). Similarly, *amīcitia* can refer to Catullus's friendship with Rufus, and it can refer also to Catullus's relationship with Lesbia, again as in Poem 109, line 6 (*amīcitiae*).

COMPREHENSION QUESTIONS

1. What things does Catullus claim Rufus has done?

2. How does Catullus characterize Rufus in lines 5–6? Cite the Latin.

CHAPTER 3

MARCUS TULLIUS CICERO

AN INTRODUCTION TO CICERO

Marcus Tullius Cicero is one of the late Roman Republic's most prolific and influential writers and intellectuals. Cicero wrote speeches; poetry; and rhetorical, philosophical, and political essays. Additionally, he left a wealth of letters that reveal his innermost thoughts, feelings, and motivations; these surviving letters, written largely in the last few years of Cicero's life, shed light on Roman society of his day and on this tumultuous and significant period of Roman history in which he actively participated.

Cicero was born to a wealthy equestrian family on the third of January 106 BCE in Arpinum, a small town sixty miles southeast of Rome. His father apparently had ambitions for his two sons, Marcus and Quintus, whom he took to Rome to further their education. Cicero studied first with the well-known orator Lucius Licinius Crassus and then with the distinguished lawyer Quintus Mucius Scaevola the Augur. Courts and assemblies served as the classrooms for young men interested in law and politics, and so Cicero learned by observation from other Roman orators and statesmen.

The quaestorship to which Cicero was elected in 76 was the first in a sequence of offices (the *cursus honōrum*) that led to the consulship. The importance of this office for Cicero was that he became the first in his family to serve in the Roman Senate; in other words, he was a *novus homō*. Cicero was elected to the office of aedile for 69 BCE and to that of praetor for 66. The pinnacle of Cicero's political career was his election to the consulship for 63 BCE. During this year Cicero successfully foiled a plot against the state. Lucius Sergius Catilina had collected a group of other disgruntled individuals and raised an army with the goal of overthrowing the government. A failed attempt on his life compelled Cicero to convene the Senate. Thereupon he delivered a brilliant speech that provided many details of the conspiracy (*In L. Catilīnam Ōrātiō Prīma*) and resulted in the desired effect of persuading Catiline to depart from Rome.

By 60 BCE Julius Caesar, Gnaeus Pompey, and Marcus Crassus had formed a political alliance (which generally is referred to as the first triumvirate). Cicero declined Caesar's repeated invitations to join this coalition as a fourth member because of his commitment to the traditional form of Roman government. The members of this alliance came to view Cicero as a threat. As a result, in 58 BCE the tribune Publius Clodius Pulcher, a supporter of Caesar and enemy of Cicero, proposed a law that would banish anyone who had executed Roman citizens without a trial. The law, which passed, would be applied retroactively. In order to avoid prosecution, Cicero set off for exile where he remained for a year and a half. The triumvirs enabled his recall from exile, something Pompey had worked tirelessly to effect. After the death of Marcus Crassus and Julia, Caesar's daughter and Pompey's wife, there was an eventual struggle for power between Caesar and Pompey. Out of personal loyalty to Pompey, Cicero joined him and his supporters against Caesar, who was victorious over Pompey at the battle of Pharsalus. Cicero and Pompey's other remaining supporters were pardoned by Caesar.

Between his return to Italy in 47 and the end of his life in 43 BCE Cicero devoted much of his time to studying and writing about philosophy. The assassination of Caesar in 44 BCE resulted in a struggle for power between Marc Antony, Marcus Aemilius Lepidus, and Octavian, Caesar's grand-nephew, adopted son, and chief heir. Cicero, hopeful that the Republic could be restored, developed a strategy to pit Antony, who was supported by Lepidus, against Octavian, a youth whose ambition and abilities Cicero underestimated. In a series of speeches known as the *Philippics*, Cicero attacked Antony, accusing him of being an enemy of the state.

Ultimately Antony, Lepidus, and Octavian met and came to an agreement to share power by creating a second triumvirate, which was legally sanctioned by the Roman Senate. They drew up a list of political enemies who would be executed and whose property would be confiscated. In light of Cicero's fourteen speeches that attacked Antony, it is not surprising that he appeared on the list of the proscribed. Attempting to escape from Italy to Macedonia, he was overtaken by Antony's soldiers at his villa at Formiae (modern-day Formia, located halfway between Rome and Naples). Cicero courageously offered his neck to his executioner who also cut off his hands. His head and hands were put on display on the speaker's platform in the Roman Forum as a warning to anyone who might oppose the members of the Second Triumvirate.

Such was the tragic end of a most brilliant orator and lawyer, a leading intellectual of his time, and a dedicated statesman who had served his country well during the course of his entire life.

READING 9

Around the time of Cicero's exile, his former protégé, Marcus Caelius Rufus, had become romantically involved with the sister of Publius Clodius Pulcher, the rich, captivating, and very aristocratic Clodia Metelli. This femme fatale enjoyed the company of men younger than herself and included among her many admirers Gaius Valerius Catullus, whose poetry memorializes his passionate and hopeless love for her (see pages 82–111 and pages 118–124 of *Latin for the New Millennium* 3). Caelius apparently had broken off the relationship with Clodia around 57 BCE. In retaliation, a year later she joined in the prosecution of Caelius, who was being arraigned on a number of counts, accusing her former lover of stealing gold from her and attempting to poison her (lines 1–17 in the first passage below). Cicero joined the team of Caelius's defenders. His speech on Caelius's behalf, in which he alleged that Clodia was the instigator of the entire case in order to take revenge on her former lover, is a work of genius that provided Cicero the opportunity to embarrass the family of his archenemy by depicting the deportment of Clodius's sister in the most scandalous terms. Cicero's strategy was successful, for Caelius was acquitted of all charges.

   M. Caelius Rufus, the defendant in Cicero's *Prō Caeliō*, is the same individual referred to as "Caelius" in Catullus's Poems 58 and 100 and as "Rufus" in Poems 59, 69, 71, and 77, one of Catullus's rivals in his poetry for the affections of Lesbia (Clodia Metelli). (For a discussion of the interrelationship among these six poems, see H. Dettmer, *Love by the Numbers: Form and Meaning in the Poetry of Catullus* [New York, 1997] 151–169.) Incidentally, the reference to poison in Catullus's Poem 77 (*nostrae crūdēle venēnum / vītae*, 5–6; *nostrae vītae* here may refer to Lesbia) appears to allude to this charge in the prosecution of Caelius. In light of the fact that we know so little about "Lesbia" (Clodia) from Catullus's poems, the information that Cicero provides about her in the *Prō Caeliō* provides us with a window into the society in which she lived.

Statue of Cicero. This statue, located in the Palace of Justice in Brussels, shows Cicero wearing the toga, the garb denoting Roman citizenship. (© 2013 Shutterstock Images, Renata Sedmakova)

CICERO DISMISSES TWO OF THE COUNTS AGAINST CAELIUS

CICERO *PRŌ CAELIŌ* 13

1   (XIII) Sunt autem duo crīmina, aurī et venēnī; in quibus ūna
atque eadem persōna versātur. Aurum sumptum ā Clōdiā,
venēnum quaesītum quod Clōdiae darētur, ut dīcitur. Omnia
sunt alia nōn crīmina sed maledicta, iurgī petulantis magis quam
5   pūblicae quaestiōnis. 'Adulter, impudīcus, sequester' convīcium
est, nōn accūsātiō. Nūllum est enim fundāmentum hōrum
crīminum, nūllae sēdēs; vōcēs sunt contumēliōsae temerē ab īrātō
accūsātōre nūllō auctōre ēmissae. (31) Hōrum duōrum crīminum

NOTES AND VOCABULARY

Line 1:   **duo, duae, duo** *card. num. adj.* two

crīmen, crīminis, n. accusation, charge, indictment; do not translate
as "crime." The word *crīmen* comes to mean "crime" only later in the
time of the Latin author Livy.

aurum, -ī, n. gold; thing(s) made of gold; gold ornaments. Just as
verbs of accusing, condemning, and acquitting take a genitive of the
charge or penalty, *crīmen,* "accusation, charge," takes a genitive that
defines the charge or accusation. So *aurī* can be translated "(one
charge) of gold" or "(a charge) involving gold." The prosecution had
(probably) contended that these gold items would be used for, or
sold to raise money for, bribes.

venēnum, -ī, n. poison

Line 2:   **īdem, eadem, idem** the same

persōna, -ae, f. person, individual

versō (1) in the passive, to be engaged in, take part in, be involved in

sūmō, sūmere, sūmpsī, sūmptum to take

ā, ab, *prep. + abl.* from, by; translate *ā* "from." Line 2 contains Cicero's
first direct mention of Clodia.

Line 3:   **quaerō, quaerere, quaesīvī, quaesītum** to seek

quī, quae, quod, *relative pron.,* which, that; *quod* introduces a relative
clause of purpose.

ut dīcitur: *ut* followed by the indicative means "as" or "when." The
phrase is here a parenthetical remark. Translate "as it is alleged."

Lines 3–4:	**omnia sunt alia:** translate "all the other things are" or "all the rest are."
Line 4:	**maledictum, -ī,** n. slander, curse
	iūrgium, -(i)ī, n. altercation, quarrel, shouting match
	petulāns, petulantis impudent
	magis quam: more than
Lines 4–5:	**iūrgī ... quaestiōnis:** genitives of description or characteristic
Line 5:	**quaestiō, quaestiōnis,** f. a seeking; investigation, judicial inquiry
	adulter, adulterī, m. illicit lover, paramour
	impudīcus, -a, -um immoral, indecent; being used substantively here, translate "pervert."
	sequester, sequestrī, m. third party acting as a depositary or escrow agent; the middleman with whom a bribe promised to a third party is left. Translate "trafficker in bribes." Note the ASYNDETON in *adulter, impudīcus, sequester.*
	convīcium, -(i)ī, n. a loud cry, shout; abuse, insult; reproach
Line 6:	**fundāmentum, -ī,** n. basis
Line 7:	**sēdēs, sēdis,** f. seat; foundation, support, basis
	vox, vōcis, f. voice, saying, word
	contumēliōsus, -a, -um abusive, insulting, outrageous, rude
	temerē, *adv.* heedlessly, recklessly
Line 8:	**accūsātor, accūsātōris,** m. accuser, prosecutor
	auctor, auctōris, m./f. originator, supporter; here translate *nūllō auctōre* as "without evidence."
	ēmittō, ēmittere, ēmīsī, ēmissum to send forth, hurl
	hōrum: picks up after the digression and refers to the first set of charges mentioned in line 1.

CICERO *PRŌ CAELIŌ* 13, CONTINUED

videō auctōrem, videō fontem, videō certum nōmen et caput.

10 Aurō opus fuit; sūmpsit ā Clōdiā, sūmpsit sine teste, habuit
quamdiū voluit. Maximum videō signum cūiusdam ēgregiae
familiāritātis. Necāre eandem voluit; quaesīvit venēnum,
sollicitāvit servōs, pōtiōnem parāvit, locum cōnstituit, clam
attulit. Magnum rūrsus ōdium videō cum crūdēlissimō discidiō

15 exstitisse. Rēs est omnis in hāc causā nōbīs, iūdicēs, cum Clōdiā,
muliere nōn sōlum nōbilī vērum etiam nōtā; dē quā ego nihil
dīcam nisi dēpellendī crīminis causā.

NOTES AND VOCABULARY

Line 9: **videō . . .videō . . .videō:** note the ANAPHORA that emphasizes these three phrases.

auctōrem: in a different sense from in the previous line. Here *auctōrem* means "originator."

fōns, fontis, m. spring, fountain, source

certus, -a, -um certain, sure, specific

nōmen, nōminis, n. name; here translate as "authority."

caput, capitis, n. head, chief, ringleader

Line 10: **opus fuit** (+ *abl.*) "there was a need for"

testis, testis, m./f. witness; a formal loan of this kind would be legally carried out with a prescribed formula and in the presence of witnesses.

habeō, habēre, habuī, habitum to have; the understood object of *habuit* is "it," referring to the gold.

Line 11: **quamdiū,** *interrog. and rel. adv.* how long?; as long as, so long as, until

maximus, -a, -um largest, greatest; here translate *maximus* "most impressive."

quīdam, quaedam, quoddam, *indefinite pron.* and *adj.,* certain

ēgregius, -a, -um uncommon, extraordinary

Line 12: **familiāritās, familiāritātis,** f. friendship, intimacy, familiarity

necō (1) to kill; note the parataxis.

īdem, eadem, idem the same

Line 13: **sollicitō** (1) to agitate, incite, bribe

pōtiō, pōtiōnis, f. a drink, potion

parō (1) to get ready, prepare

cōnstituō, cōnstituere, cōnstituī, cōnstitūtum to establish

clam, *adv.* secretly, in secret, covertly

Line 14: **adferō, adferre, attulī, adlātum** to bring or carry to a place; the understood direct object is "it," referring to the potion.

rūrsus *or* **rūrsum,** *adv.* back, backwards; on the other hand, then again

crūdēlis, -e cruel, bitter

discidium, -(i)ī, n. a tearing apart, a breakup

Line 15: **exsistō, exsistere, exstitī** to appear, arise

causa, -ae, f. cause, case

nōbīs: a dative of the person judging; this dative, which belongs to the general category of a dative of reference, is used of the person whose point of view is being expressed; here translate *nōbīs* as "in our opinion."

Line 16: **mulier, mulieris,** f. woman

nōbilis, -e known; noble, of noble birth (especially belonging to a family which had held curule magistracies). Note that *nōbilī* . . . *nōtā* form a FIGURA ETYMOLOGICA or PARONOMASIA, a figure of speech in which there is a play on two words based on their common derivation: here both *nōbilī* and *nōtā* are derived from *nōscō*.

nōtus, -a, -um well-known, notorious

Line 17: **nisi:** but for, except

dēpellō, dēpellere, dēpulī, dēpulsum to drive off, rebut, repel. *dēpellendī* is a genitive gerundive with *causā*.

causā + *gen.* for the sake of

COMPREHENSION QUESTIONS

1. What are the two counts against Caelius that Cicero describes here?

2. Who is the source of the charges?

3. What does Cicero claim is the real reason that these charges have been filed?

READING 10

In this section, Cicero reproaches Clodia, through a famous ancestor, for her scandalous behavior in being involved with a man who was not her husband.

A "RESURRECTED" DISTINGUISHED ANCESTOR UPBRAIDS CLODIA

CICERO *PRŌ CAELIŌ* 14.33–34

1   (XIV, 33) Sed tamen ex ipsā quaeram prius ūtrum mē sēcum

     sevērē et graviter et prīscē agere mālit, an remissē et lēniter et urbānē.

     Sī illō austērō mōre ac modō, aliquis mihi ab īnferīs excitandus est

     ex barbātīs illīs, nōn hāc barbulā quā ista dēlectātur sed illā horridā

5   quam in statuīs antīquīs atque imāginibus vidēmus, quī obiūrget

     mulierem et quī prō mē loquātur nē mihi ista forte suscēnseat.

NOTES AND VOCABULARY

Line 1:   **ipse, ipsa, ipsum,** *demonstrative pron.* and *adj.,* self, very

           prīus, *adv.* before, previously, first

           ūtrum, *adv.* whether; *ūtrum* introduces both direct and (as here) indirect alternative questions

           sēcum: translate "with her."

Line 2:   **sevērus, -a, -um** stern

           gravis, grave serious

           prīscus, -a, -um old, ancient, of yesteryear; translate "in a way characteristic of earlier times." Note the POLYSYNDETON in these three adverbs.

           agō, agere, ēgī, āctum to do, drive, treat; here translate "deal."

           mālō, mālle, māluī to prefer; *mālit* is present subjunctive in an indirect question.

           an, *conj.* or; *an* introduces the second possibility in an alternative indirect question.

           remissus, -a, -um relaxed

           lēnis, lēne gentle

remissē . . . urbānē: translate "in a relaxed and gentle and sophisticated way."

urbānus, -a, -um refined, sophisticated, suave

Line 3:   **austērus, -a, -um** (*of taste or smell*) harsh, severe, austere

mōs, mōris, n. custom, manner

modus, -ī, m. way, mode

aliquis, aliquid someone, something

īnferus, -a, -um lower, infernal; *hence plural substantive,* **īnferī, īnferōrum,** n. pl. the dead; regions the dead inhabit

excitō (1), to stir up, rouse, call up, raise

Line 4:   **barbātus, -a, -um** bearded; used here to indicate men who wore full beards in a time long before Cicero's own day

barbula, -ae, f. little beard, goatee; ablative of description

iste, ista, istud, *demonstrative pron.* and *adj.*, that; *ista* refers to Clodia but translate "that one."

dēlectō (1) to please, delight

horridus, -a, -um rough, scruffy, unkempt; the word "beard" is to be understood.

Line 5:   **statua, -ae,** f. statue

antīquus, -a, -um ancient, old; ancestral

imāgō, imāginis, f. image, likeness. Aristocratic families made wax death masks (called *imāginēs*) of the faces of their dead, which were kept in the atrium of the house and were carried around Rome during funeral processions.

quī: the antecedent is *aliquis*; this person will do the job on Cicero's behalf. This figure of speech is called PROSOPOPOEIA. PROSOPOPOEIA is a rhetorical figure in which either human qualities are attributed to objects or an absent or imaginary person is represented as speaking.

obiūrgō (1) to scold, chide, blame, upbraid; note the present subjunctive verb *obiūrget* that is in a relative clause of purpose.

Line 6:   **fors, fortis,** f. chance

suscēnseō, suscēnsēre, suscēnsuī (+ *dat.*) to be angry with, bear a grudge; present subjunctive in a negative clause of purpose.

CICERO *PRŌ CAELIŌ* 14.33–34, CONTINUED

Exsistat igitur ex hāc ipsā familiā aliquis ac potissimum Caecus ille;
minimum enim dolōrem capiet quī istam nōn vidēbit. Quī profectō,
sī exstiterit, sīc aget ac sīc loquētur: 'Mulier, quid tibi cum Caeliō,
10   quid cum homine adulescēntulō, quid cum aliēnō? Cūr aut
tam familiāris fuistī ut aurum commodārēs, aut tam inimīca ut
venēnum timērēs? Nōn patrem tuum vīderās, nōn patruum, nōn
avum, nōn prōavum, nōn abavum, nōn atavum audīerās cōnsulēs
fuisse; (34) nōn dēnique modo tē Q. Metellī mātrimōnium
15   tenuisse sciēbās, clārissimī ac fortissimī virī patriaeque

NOTES AND VOCABULARY

Line 7:   **exsistō, exsistere, exstitī** to come forth, appear; note the volitive use
of the present subjunctive.

familiā: often referring to the household generally; here means family
members, alive or dead.

ac potissimum: translate "and especially," "and in particular."

Caecus: refers to Appius Claudius Caecus (the Blind); Clodia and
her brother were members of the *gēns Claudia* (the Claudian clan).
Clodius is the plebeian form of the aristocratic name Claudius.
Publius Clodius Pulcher used this form of his name after he was
adopted into a plebian family in 59 BCE so that he would be eligible
to run for the office of tribune. Appius Claudius Caecus, censor in
312 BCE and consul in 307 and 296, was distinguished for a variety
of political reforms and the construction during his censorship
of the *Via Appia* (a major road going from Rome to Capua, later
to Brundisium) and the *Aqua Appia* (Rome's first aqueduct).
In 279 BCE, in advanced old age, Appius rebuked the Senate for
even considering the peace proposals of King Pyrrhus while that
adversary was on Italian soil; this speech soon became famous and
was still circulated in Cicero's day.

ille, illa, illud that; this adjective may have either a flattering
connotation of "the famous" or "well-known" or a contemptuous
connotation of "the infamous" or "so-called." Context will serve
as a guide as to whether the adjective is to be translated with this
nuance.

Line 8:	**minimus, -a, -um** smallest, least
	capiō, capere, cēpī, captum to take; here translate with *dolōrem,* "suffer."
	profectō, *adv.* truly, really, certainly
Line 9:	**aget:** translate "he will deal (with her)."
	quid . . . Caeliō: a verb must be supplied; translate "what are you doing with Caelius."
Line 10:	**adulēscentulus, -ī,** m. young man, youth
	aliēnus, -a, -um that which belongs to another; translate "a man who is not your husband."
Line 11:	**cūr,** *interrog. adv.* why?
	tam, *adv.* so, to that degree, to such a degree
	familiāris, familiāre familiar, intimate
	commodō (1) to lend, loan
	inimīcus, -a, -um unfriendly, hostile
Line 12:	**timeō, timēre, timuī** to fear, have cause to fear; be at risk from
	patruus, -ī, m. uncle; note the ASYNDETON in lines 13–15.
Line 13:	**avus, -ī,** m. grandfather, ancestor
	prōavus, -ī, m. great-grandfather
	abavus, -ī, m. great-great-grandfather
	atavus, -ī, m. great-great-great-grandfather
	cōnsul, cōnsulis, m. consul
Line 14:	**dēnique,** *adv.* finally
	modo, *adv.* recently
	tē: accusative subject of the indirect statement depending on *nōn . . . sciēbās.*
	Q. Metellī: refers to Quintus Caecilius Metellus Celer, Clodia's deceased husband, whom she had been on bad terms with and, owing to his sudden death, was rumored to have poisoned. He was a *lēgātus* to Pompey in Asia in 66 BCE, praetor in 63, when he supported Cicero, and consul in 60, when he vehemently opposed his brother-in-law, P. Clodius Pulcher. On the Senate floor, Metellus once threatened to throttle Clodius if the latter did not behave.
Lines 14–15:	**mātrimōnium, -(i)ī,** n. matrimony, wedlock; *mātrimōnium tenuisse* literally "had held the matrimony"; translate "had been the spouse."
Line 15:	**clārus, -a, -um** bright, clear, famous
	patria, -ae, f. fatherland, homeland; genitive after *amantissimī*

amantissimī, quī simul ac pedem līminī extulerat, omnīs prope
cīvīs virtūte, glōriā, dignitāte superābat? Cum ex amplissimō
genere in familiam clārissimam nūpsissēs, cūr tibi Caelius tam
coniūnctus fuit? Cognātus, adfīnis, virī tuī familiāris? Nihil
20   eōrum. Quid igitur fuit nisi quaedam temeritās ac libīdō? Nōnne
tē, sī nostrae imāginēs virīlēs nōn commovēbant, nē prōgeniēs
quidem mea, Q. illa Claudia, aemulam domesticae laudis in
glōriā muliēbrī esse admonēbat, nōn virgō illa Vestālis Claudia
quae patrem complexa triumphantem ab inimīcō tribūnō plēbēī
25   dē currū dētrahī passa nōn est? Cūr tē frāterna vitia potius quam

NOTES AND VOCABULARY

Line 16:   **amantissimus, -a, -um** most loving, most beloved, most dear

simul ac, *conj.* as soon as

pēs, pedis, m. foot; step

līmen, līminis, n. doorway, threshold; (by SYNECDOCHE) house,
home

efferō, efferre, extulī, ēlātum to carry out, set out

prope: here, an adverb "nearly," "almost"

Lines 16–17:   **omnīs . . . cīvīs:** these accusative plurals are more often seen as *omnēs
. . . cīvēs.*

Line 17:   **virtūs, virtūtis,** f. manliness, courage

glōria, -ae, f. honor, distinction

superō (1) to surpass, overcome; excel, outdo

cum, *conj.* when, since, although; translate "although."

amplus, -a, -um large, eminent, distinguished

cīvīs: note the use of the alternate accusative plural ending.

Line 18:   **genus, generis,** n. origin, family, class

nūbō, nūbere, nūpsī, nūptum to marry

Line 19:   **coniūnctus, -a, -um** connected, friendly

cognātus, -a, -um related, kindred; *hence substantive* kinsman, blood
relative

adfīnis, adfīne related by marriage; *hence substantive,* a relative by
marriage, an "in-law"

familiāris, familiaris, m./f. friend

Lines 19–20:	**nihil eōrum:** "none of these."
Line 20:	**temeritās, temeritātis,** f. rashness, recklessness, heedlessness
	libīdō, libīdinis, f. desire, passion
	nōnne: introduces a question expecting the answer "yes."
Line 21:	**virīlis, virīle** of a man, male
	commoveō, commovēre, commōvī, commōtum to move, sway
	progeniēs, progeniēī, f. offspring, descendant
Lines 21–22:	**nē . . . quidem** not even
Line 22:	**Q. illa Claudia:** idiomatic for the more standard *Q. Claudia illa. Q.* is the abbreviation for Quinta. For *illa* meaning "renowned," see line 7.
	aemulus, -a, -um vying with, rivaling; *hence substantive aemulus* or *aemula,* a rival
Line 23:	**muliēbris, muliēbre** womanly, of a woman
	admonēbat: "wasn't she a reminder for you to . . . ?"
	virgō, virginis, f. maiden; virgin; another Claudia is introduced here.
	Vestālis, Vestāle of or pertaining to Vesta, goddess of the hearth (fireplace); the six Vestal Virgins were her priestesses, serving a minimum of thirty years, after which they were permitted to marry (although they rarely did so).
Line 24:	**quae patrem complexa triumphantem:** a good example of SYNCHESIS in which the interlocked words suggest the daughter's arms around her father in an embrace.
	complector, complectī, complexus sum to embrace, hug; seize
	triumphō (1) to have a triumphal procession
	inimīcus, -a, -um unfriendly, hostile
	tribūnus, tribūnī, m. tribune, one of ten officials elected annually by the plebeians for the protection of their rights
	plēbs, plēbis *or* **plēbēs, plēbēī,** f. the common people
Line 25:	**currus, currūs,** m. chariot, triumphal chariot
	dētrahō, dētrahere, dētrāxī, dētrāctum to drag down, drag off
	patior, patī, passus sum to allow, permit; be sure to distinguish between *passus,* the last principal part of this verb, and *passus, passūs,* m. "step, pace."
	frāternus, -a, -um of or pertaining to a brother, fraternal
	vitium, vitiī, n. vice; carefully distinguish between this noun, *vitium,* and the first declension noun *vīta, -ae,* f. "life."
	potius quam: translate "rather than."

CICERO PRŌ CAELIŌ 14.33–34, CONTINUED

bona paterna et avīta et usque ā nōbīs cum in virīs tum etiam in
fēminīs repetīta mōvērunt? Ideōne ego pācem Pyrrhī dirēmī ut
tū amōrum turpissimōrum cōtīdiē foedera ferīrēs, ideō aquam
addūxī ut eā tū incestē ūterēre, ideō viam mūnīvī ut eam tū aliēnīs
30   virīs comitāta celebrārēs?'

NOTES AND VOCABULARY

Line 26:   **bona:** here, translate as "virtues."

paternus, -a, -um of or pertaining to a father, paternal

avītus, -a, -um of or pertaining to a grandfather; ancestral

usque, *adv.* as far as one can go, continuously, constantly

cum . . . tum, *conj.* both . . . and

Line 27:   **fēmina, -ae,** f. woman, wife

repetō, repetere, repetīvī, repetītum to trace back

ideō, *adv.* on that account, therefore, for that reason

pāx, pācis, f. pact, treaty; peace

Pyrrhus: (319–272 BCE) adventurer-king of Epirus (in northwestern
Greece) and ally of Tarentum in southern Italy, who made war on
Rome from 280–275 BCE

dirimō, dirimere, dirēmī, dirēmptum to pull apart, separate, break
up

Line 28:   **amor, amōris,** m. love, love affair

turpis, turpe disgraceful

foedus, foederis, n. agreement, treaty; bond

feriō, ferīre to hit, strike, blow; kill

foedus ferīre: to make a treaty, strike an agreement or bargain. Don't
confuse this fourth conjugation verb with the third conjugation
verb *ferō, ferre* "to bear, bring."

aqua, -ae, f. water; water supply, aqueduct

Line 29:   **addūcō, addūcere, addūxī, adductum** to lead toward, bring in

eā: ablative with *ūterēre*; refers to the aqueduct.

incestus, -a, -um unholy, profane; unchaste, lewd, translate *incestē* as
"in an unchaste manner."

ūterēre: *ūterēris* is the more ordinary form of this verb which uses the
alternate ending –re for –ris.

mūniō, mūnīre, mūnīvī, mūnītum to fortify; *(of roads)* build

eam: translate "it"; *eam* refers to the aqueduct.

aliēnus, -a, -um that which belongs to another

Line 30   **comitō** (1) to go along, accompany, attend

celebrō (1) to frequent

COMPREHENSION QUESTIONS

1. What reasons does Cicero give for "resurrecting" an aristocrat of old? Cite the Latin.

2. Whom does Cicero choose and why? Cite the Latin.

3. How is Quintus Metellus characterized? Cite the Latin.

4. Which female members of the Clodian family are noted as examples for Clodia to emulate?

CHAPTER 4

PUBLIUS VERGILIUS MARO

AN INTRODUCTION TO VERGIL

Vergil (Publius Vergilius Maro) was born on October 15, 70 BCE near the Italian town of Mantua in northern Italy. The ancient biographical tradition suggests that his father was rich enough to give his son an excellent education, first in Cremona and Milan and then in Rome. In the capital Vergil probably studied rhetoric and early Roman literature.

The tumultuous years following the assassination of Julius Caesar in 44 BCE were difficult ones for all Romans, and Vergil was no exception. His father probably lost his property in the land confiscated for war veterans in 41 BCE. During this period, Vergil gained the attention of the wealthy Maecenas who became the poet's patron and who introduced him to his powerful friend Octavian, later the emperor Augustus. The *Eclogues* were followed by the *Georgics*, usually described as a didactic poem on farming, published in 30 BCE. Vergil spent the next ten years working on his masterpiece, the *Aeneid*. In 19 BCE Vergil began a tour of Greece and Asia, but while in Athens the poet was persuaded by the emperor Augustus to return to Italy with him. Vergil fell ill on the return voyage and died on September 20, 19 BCE in the Italian city of Brundisium. He was buried in Naples. Vergil left instructions that if the *Aeneid* remained unfinished at his death, the epic should be burned. Augustus did not allow the poet's wishes to be carried out. The unfinished state of the manuscript is reflected in partially complete hexameter lines, which appear here and there throughout the poem.

The *Aeneid* is an epic, a long narrative poem centered on a hero. In the opening words of the poem, *arma virumque canō* ("Of the arms and man I sing"), Vergil indicates that his inspiration and model for his poetic work are the two epics of Homer. The first half of the *Aeneid*, which deals with the wanderings of Aeneas from the time he leaves Troy until he arrives in Italy, resembles Homer's *Odyssey* with its focus on the wanderings of Odysseus after the Trojan War. The second half of the *Aeneid*, with its narratives of the many battles fought by Aeneas and his men to found a home in Latium, resembles the *Iliad*. Although the *Aeneid* uses Homer's poems as a model, the epic is thoroughly Roman in thought, mood, and message.

Although the events described in the *Aeneid* take place in the distant, mythic times of the Trojan War and its aftermath, Vergil expected his audience to interpret these events through Roman eyes and through contemporary events. The hero of Vergil's epic, the Trojan Aeneas, is destined to found a city in Italy from which the Roman people will descend. The success of Aeneas means the success of Rome. Aeneas's son Ascanius, also known as Ilus or Iulus, is seen as the founder of the famous Julius *gens* ("clan"), which includes Julius Caesar and his adopted son, the emperor Augustus. Thus, the Julians could claim descent from the goddess Venus, Aeneas's mother.

The events described in the *Aeneid*, then, look ahead to later events in the history of Rome. These events include the founding of the city by Romulus, the city's prolonged rivalry with Dido's city of Carthage in the Punic Wars (264–146 BCE), and events during the Civil Wars that followed the assassination of Julius Caesar in 44 BCE, including the naval battle of Actium (31 BCE), in which the forces of Octavian defeated those of Antony and Cleopatra. The Dido depicted in the *Aeneid* is, in fact, not only the queen of Carthage, Rome's later archenemy, but is intended to call to mind the dangerous Egyptian queen Cleopatra, whom Vergil and his contemporaries feared.

Aeneas and Charon. Wenceslas Hollar (1607–1677) created this piece of art that depicts Aeneas standing next to the Sibyl who is holding the golden bough in order to gain access to Charon's skiff to cross the river Styx into the Underworld. (© Wikimedia Commons)

READING 11

Having landed in Italy after travels and adventures since leaving Troy, Aeneas and several of his men view the doors of the temple of Apollo at Cumae in Italy, which was built by Daedalus in thanksgiving for his safe escape from Crete.

AENEAS VIEWS THE MYTHOLOGICAL SCENES ON THE DOORS OF APOLLO'S TEMPLE

VERGIL *AENEID* 6.14–41

Meter: Dactylic Hexameter

> Daedalus, ut fāma est, fugiēns Mīnōïa rēgna,
>
> 15 praepetibus pennīs ausus sē crēdere caelō,
>
> īnsuētum per iter gelidās ēnāvit ad Arctōs,
>
> Chalcidicāque levis tandem super astitit arce.
>
> Redditus hīs prīmum terrīs, tibi, Phoebe, sacrāvit
>
> rēmigium ālārum, posuitque immānia templa.
>
> 20 In foribus lētum Androgeō: tum pendere poenās
>
> Cecropidae iussī—miserum!—septēna quotannīs

NOTES AND VOCABULARY

Line 14: **fāma, -ae,** f. story, fame

Mīnōïus, -a, -um of Minos; Minos was king of Crete.

Line 15: **praepes, praepetis** swift

audeō, audēre, ausus sum to dare; don't confuse this verb with *audiō, audīre, audīvī, audītum* "to hear."

crēdō, crēdere, crēdidī, crēditum (+ *dat.*) to entrust

Line 16: **īnsuētus, -a, -um** unaccustomed

ēnō (1) to swim out, fly forth

Arctus, Arctī, f. bear; "the Bears" are Ursa Major and Ursa Minor (the Big and the Little Dipper); hence *Arctī* here simply means "the North."

Chalcidicus, -a, -um Chalcidian, from Chalcis. Chalcis was the chief city on the Greek island of Euboea; the city is associated with Cumae in Italy because Cumae was founded as a colony by Greeks from Chalcis in the eighth century BCE. The EPITHET "Chalcidian" here is anachronistic, since the scene takes place in the Bronze Age, well before the Greek colonization of Italy.

levis, leve light

adsistō, adsistere, adstitī *or* **asistī** to stand near

arx, arcis, f. citadel, hilltop, summit

Line 18: **reddō, reddere, reddidī, redditum** to return, restore

Phoebe: vocative of *Phoebus*, one of Apollo's names

sacrō (1) to dedicate

Line 19: **rēmigium, -(i)ī,** n. "oarage," the act of rowing or equipment for rowing. The word is used METAPHORICALLY with *ālārum* to give the impression that Daedalus rowed through the sky with his wings.

pōnō, pōnere, posuī, positum to build, place

immānis, immāne huge, immense

Line 20: **foris, foris,** f. door (of the temple). Lines 20 and following describe the images on the doors to the temple (an ecphrasis). These images include the death of Androgeos, the urn with lots drawn, Pasiphae and the Minotaur, and the labyrinth possibly with Theseus and Ariadne.

lētum, -ī, n. death, destruction; supply *est.*

Androgeō: Greek genitive of *Androgeos*, the son of King Minos who was killed at Athens; it was for his death that Minos demanded fourteen young Athenians as food for the Minotaur.

pendere poenās: similar in meaning to *dare poenās*, "to pay the penalty."

Line 21: **Cecropidēs, -ae,** m. *lit.* descendant of Cecrops (the first king of Athens), Athenian; note the use of the patronymic. The form *Cecropidae* is nominative plural.

miserum (accusative of exclamation): pitiable (to relate)

septēnus, -a, -um seven each (i.e., seven youths and seven maidens)

quotannīs, *adv.* every year

VERGIL *AENEID* 6.14–41, CONTINUED

corpora nātōrum; stat ductīs sortibus urna.

Contrā ēlāta marī respondet Gnōsia tellūs:

hīc crūdēlis amor taurī, suppostaque fūrtō

25 Pāsiphaē, mixtumque genus prōlēsque biformis

Mīnōtaurus inest, Veneris monumenta nefandae;

hīc labor ille domūs et inextrīcābilis error;

magnum rēgīnae sed enim miserātus amōrem

Daedalus ipse dolōs tēctī ambāgēsque resolvit,

30 caeca regēns fīlō vestīgia. Tū quoque magnam

partem opere in tantō, sineret dolor, Īcare, habērēs.

NOTES AND VOCABULARY

Line 22: **nātus, -ī,** m. child

stō, stāre, stetī, statum: to stand (there); the urn with the lots drawn forms part of the scene on the door.

dūcō, dūcere, duxī, ductum to lead, draw (out); lots with names inscribed were placed in an urn. The names of seven Athenian youths and seven Athenian maidens were chosen from the urn (an ancient lottery); these individuals were sent as tribute to Crete.

sors, sortis, f. lot, destiny

Line 23: **contrā:** on the opposite side (i.e., on the other of the double doors at which Aeneas is looking.) Images of Crete balance images of Athens.

efferō, efferre, extulī, ēlātum to raise

mare, maris, n. sea; *marī* is the ablative sing. of the noun, here denoting place or separation.

respondeō, respondēre, respondī, respōnsum to correspond, balance

Gnōsius, -a, -um of Knossos, the chief city of Crete

tellūs, tellūris, f. land; note how *tellūs* is a synonym for *terra, humus,* and in some respects *patria* also.

Line 24: **taurī:** objective genitive, love *for* the bull

suppōnō, suppōnere, supposuī, suppos(i)tum to join (to the bull)

fūrtum, -ī, n. theft, secret action; translate "secretly."

Line 25:	**Pāsiphaē, Pāsiphaēs,** f. Pasiphae was the daughter of the sun god, the wife of King Minos, and the mother of the Minotaur.

genus, generis, n. offspring; distinguish carefully between *genus, generis* and *gēns, gentis,* f. "family, clan."

prōlēs, prōlis, f. offspring, progeny

biformis, biforme two-formed, two-shaped

Line 26:   **insum, inesse, infuī** to be in or on (the doors)

Veneris . . . nefandae: Pasiphae fell in love with the handsome bull because of the anger of either Venus or Neptune.

monumentum, -ī, n. monument, remembrance, reminder

nefandus, -a, -um unspeakable, evil

Line 27:   **domūs:** genitive with *labor; ille* could be construed as a TRANSFERRED EPITHET, modifying *domūs:* "Labor of that famous construction (i.e., the labyrinth) . . . ." The genitive *domūs* also could be construed as in apposition to *labor,* with the phrase translated as "that famous house, product of [great] labor."

inextrīcābilis, inextrīcābile impossible to find one's way out

error, errōris, m. wandering; i.e., of the labyrinth

Line 28:   **magnum:** modifies *amōrem.*

rēgīnae: Here the word, referring to Ariadne, means "princess," and not "queen." Ariadne, Minos and Pasiphae's daughter, fell in love with the Athenian prince Theseus, and begged Daedalus to help him to escape the Labyrinth. Daedalus gave him a ball of string that Theseus used to mark his path and find his way out of the Labyrinth after he killed the Minotaur.

sed enim, *conj.* but in fact; translate this phrase first.

miseror (1) to pity

Line 29:   **dolus, -ī,** m. trick

ambāges, ambāgis, f. winding, evasion

resolvō, resolvere, resolvī, resolūtum to solve

Line 30:   **caecus, -a, -um** blind

regō, regere, rēxī, rēctum to direct, guide

fīlum, -ī, n. thread, string; be careful to distinguish between *fīlius,* "son" and *fīlum,* "thread."

vestīgium, -(i)ī, n. step, walking

Line 31:   **opus, operis,** n. work

sineret: conditional use of the subjunctive with *sī* suppressed: "If grief allowed . . . ." *Sineret . . . habērēs* form a present contrary to fact condition, as do *perlegerent . . . adforet* in lines 34–35.

VERGIL *AENEID* 6.14–41, CONTINUED

Bis cōnātus erat cāsūs effingere in aurō,

bis patriae cecidēre manūs. Quīn prōtinus omnia

perlegerent oculīs, nī iam praemissus Achātēs

35 adforet atque ūnā Phoebī Triviaeque sacerdōs,

Dēiphobē Glaucī, fātur quae tālia rēgī:

"Nōn hoc ista sibī tempus spectācula poscit;

nunc grege dē intāctō septem mactāre iuvencōs

praestiterit, totidem lēctās dē mōre bidentēs."

40 Talibus adfāta Aenēān (nec sacra morantur

iussa virī) Teucrōs vocat alta in templa sacerdōs.

NOTES AND VOCABULARY

Line 32: **cāsūs:** "fall"; poetic use of the plural for singular.

effingō, effingere, effixī, effixum to express, portray

aurum, -ī, n. gold; don't confuse this noun with the third declension noun *auris, auris,* f. "ear" or with the first declension noun *aura, -ae,* f. "breeze."

Line 33: **patrius, -a, -um** paternal, of the father; this word scans *pa + tri + ae* here, and so the first syllable is short.

cecidēre: note the use of the contracted form of *cedidērunt* from *cadō.*

quīn: "Yes, he even . . ." "Why, he even" (In prose, this construction usually reads *quīn etiam.*)

prōtinus, *adv.* successively

omnia: here, for the sake of the meter, the word scans *omn-ja* (2 syllables).

Line 34: **perlegō, perlegere, perlēgī, perlēctum** to scan, survey; Aeneas and several of his men are serving as the subject of the plural verb.

nī = *nisi* if not

Achātēs: Achates, Aeneas's closest friend among his Trojan followers.

Line 35: **adforet:** third singular imperfect subjunctive from *adsum,* to be present, arrive

ūnā, *adv.* together, at the same time

Trivia, -ae, f. *lit.* "she of the fork in the road," an EPITHET of the goddess Diana, Apollo's twin sister

sacerdōs, sacerdōtis, m./f. priest, priestess; here, the Sybil

Line 36:	**Glaucī:** understand *fīlia*, "the daughter of Glaucus"
	quae: this line has a very convoluted word order. The *quae* refers to the Sybil, and has been displaced from the beginning of its relative clause. The subject of *fātur* is *quae*, and the object of *fātur*, *tālia*; *rēgī*, which refers to Aeneas, is an indirect object.
Line 37:	**hoc:** pronounced *hocc* here, thus making the "o" of *hoc* long.
	ista: those, i.e., that at which you are looking
	tempus, temporis, n. time; here, the current time or moment
	spectāculum, -ī, n. sight, spectacle
	poscō, poscere, poposcī to demand, require
Line 38:	**grege . . . intāctō:** an *intāctus* ("untouched") victim is one that has never been placed under a yoke.
	iuvencus, -ī, m. bull calf; steer
Line 39:	**praestiterit:** impersonal perfect subjunctive from *praestō*, to be superior; translate "it would be better . . . ."
	lēctās: perfect passive participle from *legō* "to choose"
	dē mōre: according to custom
	bidēns, bidentis sheep
Line 40:	**tālis, tāle** such; supply *dictīs* with *talibus*.
	adfor (1) to address
	sacrum, -ī, n. (in pl.) rituals
Line 41:	**Teucer, Teucrī,** m. Trojan; remember that *Teucer* is a synonym of *Troiānus* and *Dardan(i)us*.

COMPREHENSION QUESTIONS

1. What did Daedalus succeed in escaping? Cite the Latin.

2. What did Daedalus sacrifice and to whom?

3. What scene did Aeneas first see on the doors of the temple?

4. What in particular did Daedalus find difficult to engrave on the doors? Cite the Latin.

5. What types of animals and how many was Aeneas told to sacrifice?

READING 12

At the request of his dead father Anchises, Aeneas seeks out the Sibyl in Cumae and persuades her to lead him to the Underworld to visit his father. In his tour of the Underworld Aeneas recognizes Dido in the group of shades who have died for love. Aeneas addresses her lovingly, explaining that he left her unwillingly. Dido responds by ignoring him and walking away. Aeneas is shaken by the realization that he caused her death.

AENEAS VISITS THE UNDERWORLD

VERGIL *AENEID* 6.450–476

Meter: Dactylic Hexameter

450 Inter quās Phoenissa recēns ā vulnere Dīdō

errābat silvā in magnā; quam Trōius hērōs

ut prīmum iuxtā stetit agnōvitque per umbrās

obscūram, quālem prīmō quī surgere mēnse

aut videt aut vīdisse putat per nūbila lūnam,

455 dēmīsit lacrimās dulcīque adfātus amōre est:

"Īnfēlīx Dīdō, vērus mihi nuntius ergō

vēnerat exstīnctam ferrōque extrēma secūtam?

Fūneris heu tibi causa fuī? Per sīdera iūrō,

per superōs et sī qua fidēs tellūre sub īmā est,

460 invītus, rēgīna, tuō dē lītore cessī.

NOTES AND VOCABULARY

Line 450:   **inter quās:** translate *quās* as a demonstrative "these women." Dido is the last in a list of mythical females about whose sad deaths we are reminded as Aeneas observes them in the underworld. The list includes Phaedra, Procris, Pasiphae, and Laodamia.

Phoenissa, -ae, f. Phoenician (woman), Dido

recēns, recentis recent, fresh; *recēns ā vulnere = recentī vulnere* ("with a fresh wound") would be more natural in English; but Vergil wants to emphasize not only the freshness of Dido's wound, but also her very recent arrival in the underworld.

vulnus, vulneris, n. wound, deadly blow

Line 451:	**Trōius, -a, -um** Trojan, of Troy
	hērōs, hērōis, m. hero, mighty warrior
Line 452:	**iuxtā,** *adv.* near, next; *prep. + acc.* close to; take *quam* (line 451) both with *iuxtā* and with *agnōvit* in line 452.
	agnōscō, agnōscere, agnōvī, agnitum to recognize
Line 453:	**obscūrus, -a, -um** dark, obscure, dim (literally, *obscūram* is modifying an understood *umbram*.)
	quālis, quāle (such) as, of what sort; this SIMILE comparing Dido to the elusive new (crescent) moon merits comparison to the SIMILE with which we (and Aeneas) were introduced to her at 1.498–502. Note the HYPERBATON in *quālem . . . lūnam*, which emphasizes *lūnam*.
	quī = *aliquī* translate "someone."
	mēnsis, mēnsis, m. month
Line 454:	**putō** (1) to think, suppose, consider
	nūbilum, -ī, n. cloud, cloudiness
	lūna, -ae, f. moon, moonlight
Line 455:	**dēmittō, dēmittere, dēmīsī, dēmissum** to send down, let fall, drop, lower
	dulcis, dulce sweet, dear, fond
	adfor (1) to address, accost
	amōre: ablative of manner
Line 456:	**vērus, -a, -um** true, real, genuine
	nuntius, -(i)ī, m. messenger, message
	ergō, *adv.* therefore, then, consequently
Line 457:	**exstinguō, exstinguere, exstīnxī, exstīnctum** to quench, destroy, extinguish; (*tē*) *exstīnctam* (*esse*).
	extrēma, extrēmōrum, n. pl. end, death, funeral; *extrēma* (= *mortem*) *secūtam* (*esse*). The noun *extrēma*, "end," is a EUPHEMISM here for "death."
Line 458:	**fūnus, fūneris,** n. funeral, death, disaster
	causa, -ae, f. cause, reason, occasion
	iūrō (1) to swear (by), take oath
Line 459:	**fidēs, fideī,** f. faith, honor, pledge
Line 460:	**invītus, -a, -um** unwilling, reluctant
	cēdō, cēdere, cessī, cessum to yield, depart

VERGIL *AENEID* 6.450–476, CONTINUED

Sed mē iussa deum, quae nunc hās īre per umbrās,

per loca senta sitū cōgunt noctemque profundam,

imperiīs ēgēre suīs; nec crēdere quīvī

hunc tantum tibi mē discessū ferre dolōrem.

465   Siste gradum tēque aspectū nē subtrahe nostrō.

Quem fugis? Extrēmum fātō quod tē adloquor hoc est."

Tālibus Aenēās ardentem et torva tuentem

lēnībat dictīs animum lacrimāsque ciēbat.

Illa solō fīxōs oculōs āversa tenēbat

470   nec magis inceptō vultum sermōne movētur

quam sī dūra silex aut stet Marpēsia cautēs.

NOTES AND VOCABULARY

Line 461:   **iussum, -ī,** n. command, order, behest; note the syncopation of *deōrum.*

Line 462:   **sentus, -a, -um** rough, thorny

      situs, sitūs, m. position; neglect; decay

      cōgō, cōgere, coēgī, coāctum to force (together), compel

      profundus, -a, -um deep, profound, vast

Line 463:   **crēdō, crēdere, crēdidī, crēditum** (+ *dat.*) to believe, trust

      queō, quīre, quīvī (-iī), quītum to be able, can

Line 464:   **discessus, discessūs,** m. departure, separation

      dolor, dolōris, m. grief, pain, passion, anger

Line 465:   **sistō, sistere, stitī, statum** to stay, stop

      gradus, gradūs, m. step, gait, pace, stride

      a(d)spectus, a(d)spectūs, m. sight, vision, aspect

      subtrahō, subtrahere, subtrāxī, subtractum to withdraw

Line 466:   **Extrēmum fātō quod tē adloquor hoc est:** translate "this is the last (word, or speech), because of fate, which I shall address to you."

      adloquor, adloquī, adlocūtus sum to address, accost

      hoc est: pronounce *hocc*, making a long syllable; it is unusual, to say the least, to conclude a line with two monosyllables; their appearance here, though perhaps inelegant, is certainly emphatic.

Line 467:	**torvus, -a, -um** fierce, grim, lowering; *torva*: neuter accusative plural used adverbially, probably in imitation of the similar Greek construction.
	tueor, tuērī, tuitus (tūtus) sum to look (at), watch
Lines 467–468:	**tuentem . . . animum:** the expression is unusually contorted—how can one's mind or anger be imagined as watching? Vergil implies that Dido is effectively consumed by her anger—it is all that remains of her. Note the HYPERBATON, *tālibus . . . dictīs*, which emphasizes "words."
Line 468:	**lēniō, lēnīre, lēnīvī, lēnītum** to soften, soothe, calm; *lēnībat* = *lēniēbat*, which could not be used in hexameter. It has a conative meaning here, "he tried to soothe."
	cieō, ciēre, cīvī, citum to stir (up), (a)rouse
Line 469:	**solum, -ī,** n. ground, earth, soil
	fīgō, fīgere, fīxī, fīxum to fasten, fix, pierce
	āvertō, āvertere, āvertī, āversum to turn away, avert
Line 470:	**magis,** *adv.* more, rather
	incipiō, incipere, incēpī, inceptum to begin, undertake
	vultus, vultūs, m. countenance, face, aspect; *vultum* is an accusative of respect or an accusative direct object with middle/reflexive verb *movētur*.
	sermō, sermōnis, m. conversation, speech; *sermōne*: the word is ironic, since it suggests conversation; yet Dido does not respond.
Line 471:	**quam,** *adv.* how, than
	dūrus, -a, -um hard(y), harsh, stern
	silex, silicis, m./f. flint, rock, crag
	Marpēs(s)ius, -a, -um of Marpe(s)sus; *Marpēsia cautēs*: Marpessus, a mountain on the Greek island of Paros, was renowned as a source of fine marble for sculpture.
	cautēs, cautis, f. rock, cliff, crag; note the SIMILE.

VERGIL *AENEID* 6.450–476, CONTINUED

Tandem corripuit sēsē atque inimīca refūgit

in nemus umbriferum, coniūnx ubi prīstinus illī

respondet cūrīs aequatque Sychaeus amōrem.

475 Nec minus Aenēās cāsū concussus inīquō

prōsequitur lacrimīs longē et miserātur euntem.

NOTES AND VOCABULARY

Line 472:   **corripiō, corripere, corripuī, correptum** to snatch (up, away)

inimīcus, -a, -um hostile, unfriendly

refugiō, refugere, refūgī to flee (away), withdraw, shun

Line 473:   **nemus, nemoris,** n. (sacred) grove, forest

umbrifer, umbrifera, umbriferum shady; shade-bearing; the double meaning is active here: the underworld is filled with both gloom and the shades of the dead.

ubi: the conjunction has been postponed.

prīstinus, -a, -um ancient, former

illī: dative of reference

Line 474:   **respondeō, respondēre, respondī, respōnsum** to answer, sympathize with

cūra, -ae, f. pain, sorrow

aequō (1) to equal(ize), match, reciprocate, level

Sychaeus, -ī, m. deceased husband of Dido

Line 475:   **minus,** *adv.* less

cāsus, cāsūs, m. chance, (mis)fortune; *cāsū (Dīdōnis)*

concutiō, concutere, concussī, concussum to shake, shatter, agitate

inīquus, -a, -um unjust, harsh, uneven

Line 476:   **prōsequor, prōsequī, prōsecūtus sum** to follow, attend; *prōsequitur et miserātur (eam).*

longē, *adv.* (from) afar, at a distance

miseror (1) to pity, commiserate

COMPREHENSION QUESTIONS

1. Where was Dido in the Underworld when Aeneas first caught sight of her?

2. According to what Aeneas says in this passage, why did he leave Carthage? Cite the Latin.

3. How did Dido react to what Aeneas just told her? Cite the Latin.

4. To whom did Dido flee after Aeneas finished speaking?

READING 13

Accompanied by the Sibyl, Aeneas meets his deceased father Anchises, who predicts the areas in which Rome will excel and identifies for him unborn souls as future Roman heroes. Anchises's praise of the accomplishments of the elder Marcellus effects a transition to his tribute to the younger Marcellus, the nephew, adopted son, and intended heir of Augustus, and who, unfortunately, died at the age of 19. Aeneas and the Sibyl leave the Underworld through the gate of ivory.

ANCHISES SPEAKS TO AENEAS IN THE UNDERWORLD

VERGIL *AENEID* 6.847–866, 893–899

Meter: Dactylic Hexameter

"Excūdent aliī spīrantia mollius aera

(crēdō equidem), vīvōs dūcent dē marmore vultūs,

ōrābunt causās melius, caelīque meātūs

850 dēscrībent radiō et surgentia sīdera dīcent:

tū regere imperiō populōs, Rōmāne, mementō

(hae tibi erunt artēs), pācīque impōnere mōrem,

parcere subiectīs et dēbellāre superbōs."

Sīc pater Anchīsēs, atque haec mīrantibus addit:

NOTES AND VOCABULARY

Line 847:   **excūdō, excūdere, excūdī, excūsum** to hammer out, fashion;
Anchises uses the future tense repeatedly in this passage, to
describe the great moments in the history of a people that does not
yet exist. The passage that begins in line 847 is proleptic—that is,
it looks forward in time and outside the frame of the rest of the tale
told in the *Aeneid* as a whole. This instance of prolepsis is worth
considering from several perspectives: from the point of view of
both Anchises and Aeneas, the events and characters foretold do
not yet exist except as a promise of the fates; from the point of view
of Vergil and his readers, these events and characters are already
reflections of the past.

aliī: the implied reference here is to the Greeks, whose accomplishments in sculpture, rhetoric, and the sciences are guaranteed by Anchises's prescience.

spīrō (1) to breathe, blow, live, quiver; *spīrantia aera*: bronze statues so lifelike that they seem to breathe. Note the PERSONIFICATION here.

mollis, molle soft, gentle, graceful

aes, aeris, n. bronze

Line 848:   **crēdō, crēdere, crēdidī, crēditum** to believe, suppose

equidem, *adv.* indeed, truly, surely

vīvus, -a, -um living, alive, natural, lifelike

marmor, marmoris, n. marble

vultus, vultūs, m. countenance, face, aspect

Line 849:   **ōrō** (1) to pray (for), entreat, plead, argue

causa, -ae, f. cause, case (at law)

melior, melius better, superior, finer

meātus, meātūs, m. course, path, motion

Line 850:   **dēscrībō, dēscrībere, dēscripsī, dēscriptum** to mark out, map

radius, -(i)ī, m. rod, spoke, compass

dīcent = *vocābunt*

Line 851:   **regō, regere, rēxī, rēctum** to rule, guide, direct

populus, -ī, m. people, nation

Rōmānus, -a, -um Roman, of Rome; *Rōmāne*: addressed to the Roman people in general, and to Aeneas in particular—he represents the people whose nation and identity do not yet exist, but are assured by the fates.

Line 852:   **pāx, pācis,** f. peace, quiet, repose

impōnō, imponere, imposuī, impositum to place on, impose, establish

mōs, mōris, m. custom, usage, rule, law; be careful to distinguish between *mōs, mōris* and *mora, -ae,* f. "delay."

Line 853:   **parcō, parcere, pepercī (parsī) parsum** (+ *dat.*) to spare

subiciō, subicere, subiēcī, subiectum to vanquish

dēbellō (1) to exhaust through war, crush

superbus, -a, -um proud, haughty

Line 854:   **pater Anchīsēs:** supply *dīxit*.

mīrantibus: refers to Aeneas and the Sibyl.

addō, addere, addidī, additum to add

VERGIL *AENEID* 6.847–866, 893–899, CONTINUED

855 "Aspice, ut īnsignis spoliīs Mārcellus opīmīs

ingreditur victorque virōs superēminet omnēs.

Hic rem Rōmānam magnō turbante tumultū

sistet eques, sternet Poenōs Gallumque rebellem,

tertiaque arma patrī suspendet capta Quirīnō."

860 Atque hīc Aenēās (ūnā namque īre vidēbat

ēgrēgium formā iuvenem et fulgentibus armīs,

sed frōns laeta parum et dēiectō lūmina vultū)

NOTES AND VOCABULARY

Line 855:   **a(d)spiciō, a(d)spicere, a(d)spexī** to see, look at

īnsignis, īnsigne distinguished, marked, noteworthy

spolium, -(i)ī, n. spoil, booty, plunder

Mārcellus, -ī, m. Marcus Claudius Marcellus, d. 208 BCE; famous
Roman consul, served in both the First and Second Punic Wars;
was an outstanding general in the Second Punic War, and was an
ancestor of the younger Marcellus.

opīmus, -a, -um rich, splendid, sumptuous; *spolia opīma,* "spoils of
honor"; *spoliīs opīmīs* is the technical term in Latin for arms and
other booty taken on the field of battle by the victorious general
from the vanquished general, whom he has slain with his own hand.
These were won before by Romulus early in his kingship and by
Cossus in 428 BCE (the latter of these is mentioned at line 841), and
finally by the elder Marcellus in 222 BCE. When Augustus came to
power, he decreed that, since he had *imperium* and was effectively
commander-in-chief, only he and his successors could claim the
honor henceforth.

Line 856:   **ingredior, ingredī, ingressus sum** to step, stride, enter

superēmineō, superēminēre to tower above, surpass

Line 857:   **turbō** (1) to confuse, shake, disturb

tumultus, tumultūs, m. tumult, uprising, clamor; the war with the
Gauls in Italy, in which the elder Marcellus had killed Viridomarus,
leader of the Gauls, at Clastidium (222 BCE), and stripping him of
his armor had obtained the third and last *spolia opīma* (the *tertia
arma capta* of 859).

Line 858:	**sistō, sistere, stitī, statum** to stop, to cause to stand firm
	eques, equitis, m. cavalryman, knight, man of equestrian rank; "(though but) a man of equestrian rank"; the term also serves as a reminder that the battle of Clastidium was waged by cavalry.
	sternō, sternere, strāvī, strātum to lay low, strew
	Poenus, -a, -um Phoenician, Carthaginian
	Gallus, -a, -um Gallic, Gaul
	rebellis, rebelle rebellious, insurgent
Line 859:	**tertius, -a, -um** third
	suspendō, suspendere, suspendī, suspēnsum to hang up; Vergil introduces another technical term, here part of the vocabulary for making a dedication of spoils to a god by hanging them in (or on) the temple.
	Quirīnus, -ī, m. the deified Romulus as god of war. The name *Quirīnō* comes as something of a surprise, since the *spolia opīma* were traditionally dedicated not to Quirinus but to Jupiter Feretrius. It is not wise to suppose, however, as some commentators have done, that Vergil was confused; it is far more likely that this alteration serves a purpose here—perhaps to bring special honor to Romulus, who as the first winner of *spolia opīma* began the tradition of dedication to Jupiter Feretrius; since upon his death Romulus was deified as Quirinus, Vergil may well intend to remind us here of both divinities associated with the ritual, especially since Augustus's lineage takes him back to Romulus as well as Aeneas.
Line 860:	**ūnā,** *adv.* together, at the same time; *ūnā (cum Mārcellō).*
Line 861:	**ēgregius, -a, -um** extraordinary, distinguished
	forma, -ae, f. form, beauty, shape, appearance
	iuvenis, iuvenis, m./f. youth, young man, young woman
	fulg(e)ō, fulgēre (-ere), fulsī to shine, gleam, glitter
Line 862:	**frōns, frontis,** f. front, forehead, brow; understand *erat* with *frōns.*
	parum, *adv.* slightly, too little, not
	dēiciō, dēicere, dēiēcī, dēiectum to cast down; *dēiectō vultū* is an ablative of description, and is equivalent in meaning to *et lūmina (erant) dēiecta.* The word *lūmina* here signifies *oculī,* as often.
	vultus, vultūs, m. countenance, face, aspect

VERGIL *AENEID* 6.847–866, 893–899, CONTINUED

"Quis, pater, ille, virum quī sīc comitātur euntem?

Fīlius, anne aliquis magnā dē stirpe nepōtum?

865 Quī strepitus circā comitum! Quantum īnstar in ipsō!

Sed nox ātra caput tristī circumvolat umbrā."

Lines 867–886 are concerned with the early and untimely death of Marcellus. In the closing lines of Book 6, Anchises accompanies Aeneas and the Sibyl to the gates leading out of the Underworld.

Sunt geminae Somnī portae, quārum altera fertur

cornea, quā vērīs facilis datur exitus umbrīs,

895 altera candentī perfecta nitēns elephantō,

sed falsa ad caelum mittunt īnsomnia Mānēs.

NOTES AND VOCABULARY

Line 863: **ille:** the younger M. Claudius Marcellus, i.e., the son of Augustus's sister Octavia and husband of Augustus's daughter Julia; born in 42 BCE. Augustus had chosen him to be his successor, but he died in 23 BCE.

virum: i.e., the elder Marcellus.

comitor (1) to accompany, attend, escort, follow

Line 864: **an(ne),** *interrog.* whether, or

aliquis, aliquid some(one), any(one)

stirps, stirpis, f. stock, lineage, race

nepōs, nepōtis, m. grandson; descendant; *nepōtum (nostrōrum).*

Line 865: **strepitus, strepitūs,** m. uproar, noise, clamor; *strepitus* indicates the future fame and popularity of the younger Marcellus.

circā, *adv.* around, about

quantus, -a, -um so (much, great, many), as

īnstar, n. *indecl.* likeness, presence, weight, dignity

Line 866: **circumvolō** (1) to fly around, fly about

Line 893: **Somnus, -ī,** m. Sleep, Slumber personified as a divinity

porta, -ae, f. gate; this first declension noun should not be confused with *portus, portūs,* m., a fourth declension noun that means "harbor" or with the verb *portō* (1) "to carry."

alter, altera, alterum one (of two); *alter* in line 895 coordinates with *alter* in line 893. Translate "the one . . . the other."

fertur (esse) = *dīcitur (esse).* Again Vergil implies that the two gates from the Underworld are part of a tradition already known to his readers: in this case, first and foremost from Homer, who describes the two Gates of Dreams in *Odyssey* 19.562–567.

Line 894: **corneus, -a, -um** of horn

vērus, -a, -um true, real, genuine, honest

facilis, facile easy, favorable, ready

exitus, exitūs, m. exit, outlet, egress

Line 895: **candēns, candentis** shining, white, gleaming; *candentī elephantō*: ablative of material. The ablative of material can indicate the source of which something is made of.

perficiō, perficere, perfēcī, perfectum to finish, make

nitēns, nitentis gleaming, bright, shining

elephantus, -ī, m. elephant, ivory

Line 896: **falsus, -a, -um** false, deceitful, mock

īnsomnium, -(i)ī, n. dream, vision

Mānēs, Mānium, m. (souls of) the dead, Hades

VERGIL *AENEID* 6.847–866, 893–899, CONTINUED

Hīs ibi tum nātum Anchīsēs ūnāque Sibyllam

prōsequitur dictīs portāque ēmittit eburnā;

ille viam secat ad nāvēs sociōsque revīsit.

NOTES AND VOCABULARY

Line 897:   **ibi,** *adv.* there, then

ūnā, *adv.* together, at the same time

Sibylla, -ae, f. ancient Italian prophetess

Line 898:   **prōsequor, prōsequī, prōsecūtus sum** to follow, escort

ēmittō, emittere, emīsī, emissum to send forth

eburnus, -a, -um (of) ivory

Line 899:   **ille:** refers to Aeneas.

secō, secāre, secuī, sectum to cut, cleave; pass through

revīsō, revisere to revisit, see again

COMPREHENSION QUESTIONS

1. To whom do the *aliī* that Anchises mentions in line 847 refer?

2. List at least three areas in which the *aliī* will excel over the Romans. Cite the Latin.

3. What does Anchises say the great skill of the Romans will be?

4. For what was the elder Marcellus famous? Cite the Latin.

5. Of what materials are the twin gates of Sleep made? From which gate does Aeneas exit?

CHAPTER 5

QUINTUS HORATIUS FLACCUS

AN INTRODUCTION TO HORACE

Horace, one of Augustan Rome's greatest poets, wrote at a time that included great political upheaval and great literary achievement. His two books of *Satires,* or "Conversations," served as a model and inspiration for later Roman and English satirists. His lyric poems were so extraordinary that few Latin poets after Horace attempted to write lyric. Horace's lyric poems were quite popular in the sixteenth and seventeenth centuries and were translated and widely imitated by English, French, Spanish, and Italian poets of that era. His *Ars Poētica,* a work on poetic composition, was profoundly influential for western writers from the seventeenth century and beyond. Further, Horace's verve at creating memorable maxims has had a lasting impact on our own language. Horace would be quite surprised, for example, at the popularity even today of his brilliantly coined phrase, *carpe diem.*

Quintus Horatius Flaccus was born on December 8, 65 BCE, in the town of Venusia (modern Venosa), located on the border between Apulia and Lucania in southern Italy. He was the son of a freedman, or an ex-slave, who worked as an auction agent or *coāctor argentārius.* Nothing is known of Horace's mother. Despite his social status Horace's father must have had sufficient resources to provide his son with the kind of education typical for those from families of the equestrian or senatorial class. His father took him to Rome for his early education and later sent him to Athens in 44 BCE to pursue studies in philosophy. There Horace made the acquaintance of Cicero's son Marcus. Later that year Brutus, one of the assassins of Julius Caesar, recruited both Horace and Marcus to join the cause of reestablishing the Roman Republic. Horace fought on the losing side at the battle of Philippi in 42 BCE, which secured the defeat of the republican cause and the victory of Antony and Octavian, the heirs to Caesar's power. After Octavian declared an amnesty for all who had fought against him, Horace returned to Italy.

Horace wrote poetry over a period of about thirty years. His first publication in 35 BCE was Book 1 of the *Satires* or *Sermōnēs* ("Conversations"), followed five years later by Book 2. Latin satire is verse in a conversational style on a variety of topics written from an individual point of view. Horace's satires, composed in dactylic hexameter, touch on a variety of literary, social, and ethical topics and include humorous or playful attacks on various human faults. Like the *Satires,* the *Epodes,* or *Iambī* as they are sometimes called, were written early in Horace's career. These poems follow in the tradition of the early Greek poet Archilochus of Paros, who wrote poems of attack and blame. In 23 BCE Horace published Books 1 through 3 of his collection of lyric poetry, the *Odes* or *Carmina.* He returned to lyric ten years later and published Book 4 of the *Odes,* which includes much that is in praise of Augustus. The odes range widely in subject matter and include the themes of politics, love, literature, death's inevitability, life's brevity, friendship, and more. The personal is often mixed with the public. While Horace was self-consciously writing in a long literary tradition that included much Greek influence, his poems are very contemporary. In addition to the Roman political world that pervades the *Odes,* the social environment Horace inhabited is evident.

Temple of Castor and Pollux. In *Odes* 1.3, Horace appeals to many powers, including the Dioscuri, to help keep Vergil safe on his journey to Greece. The Dioscuri were known in both Greece and Rome as saviors in a variety of spheres. The temple in the Roman forum was built in 484 BCE to honor their epiphany at Lake Regillus, the site of a heroic victory over the Latins in 499 or 496 BCE, as discussed by Cicero in *De Natura Deorum* 2.6. The temple was restored several times over the years including in 6 CE by the Emperor Tiberius. Nearby is the Lacus of Juturna where the equestrian duo, according to tradition, watered their horses. (© 2013 Shutterstock Images LLC)

READING 14

Horace wishes Vergil safe travel on the sea by addressing the ship that is transporting him and laments human innovation that made such travel possible.

VERGIL'S VOYAGE TO GREECE

HORACE *ODES* 1.3

Meter: Second Asclepiad

1   Sīc tē dīva potēns Cyprī,

      sīc frātrēs Helenae, lūcida sīdera,

         ventōrumque regat pater

      obstrictīs aliīs praeter Iāpyga,

5   nāvis, quae tibi crēditum

      dēbēs Vergilium: fīnibus Atticīs

         reddās incolumem precor

      et servēs animae dīmidium meae.

NOTES AND VOCABULARY

Line 1:   **sīc** thus, so; this idiomatic use of *sīc* in a wish is practically untranslatable; note the ANAPHORA of *sīc* in lines 1 and 2.

        tē: refers to the ship

        dīva, -ae, f. goddess

        potēns, potentis powerful, mighty

        Cyprus, -ī, f. Cyprus, an island sacred to the goddess Aphrodite/ Venus; since she was born from the sea, the goddess was considered a patron of sailors.

Line 2:   **frātrēs Helenae:** refers to Castor and Pollux, the twin brothers of Helen of Troy. After their death it was believed that they became St. Elmo's fire, and were thus considered patrons of mariners. They were also identified with the constellation Gemini.

        lūcidus, -a, -um bright

        sīdus, sīderis, n. star, planet

Line 3:   **ventōrum pater:** refers to Aeolus, the god who rules over the winds.

regō, regere, rēxī, rēctum to guide; *dīva, frātrēs,* and *pater* are all subjects of this verb being used as a volitive subjunctive. *Regat* agrees with the nearest subject. Be careful not to confuse the verb *regō* with the verb *rēgnō* nor with the noun *rēx, rēgis.*

Line 4:   **obstringō, obstringere, obstrinxī, obstrictum** to hold in check, confine

aliīs: refers to *ventīs; ventīs obstrictīs* is an ablative absolute.

praeter, *prep. + acc.* except

Iāpyx (3 syllables), **Iāpygis,** m. north-by-northwest wind; note the accusative singular Greek ending. This wind facilitates the crossing from Italy to Greece by way of the Ionian Sea.

Lines 5–8:   **crēditum, dēbēs,** and **reddās:** these verbs involve several METAPHORS from banking.

Line 5:   **nāvis:** vocative case

crēdō, crēdere, crēdidī, crēditum to trust, entrust; translate *crēditum* "having been lent."

Line 6:   **dēbeō, dēbēre, dēbuī, dēbitum** to be under an obligation, owe; remember that *dēbeō* used with an infinitive has the quite different meaning of "ought, should."

Vergilium: refers to P(ublius) Vergilius Maro, the poet Vergil

fīnibus: dative with *reddās* in line 7

Atticus, -a, -um Attic, of the region of Attica, which surrounds the Greek city of Athens.

Line 7:   **reddō, reddere, reddidī, redditum** to return, restore, deliver

incolumis, incolumne safe, sound, unharmed

precor (1) pray, beg; the verb is governing *reddās* and *servēs,* with an ELLIPSIS of *ut* in an indirect command.

Line 8:   **servō** (1) to save, preserve. Be careful not to confuse the verb *servō* with the verb *serviō,* "to serve."

anima, -ae, f. soul, life, spirit; *animae dīmidium meae* is a common sentiment in Roman literature: a close friend is a "second self" or "half of oneself." *Animus,* "mind," belongs to the same word family as *anima.*

dīmidium, -(i)ī, n. one-half

HORACE *ODES* 1.3, CONTINUED

      illī rōbur et aes triplex

10 circā pectus erat, quī fragilem trucī

      commīsit pelagō ratem

prīmus, nec timuit praecipitem Āfricum

      dēcertantem Aquilōnibus

nec trīstīs Hyadas nec rabiem Notī,

15   quō nōn arbiter Hadriae

māior, tollere seu pōnere volt freta.

      quem mortis timuit gradum

quī siccīs oculīs mōnstra natantia,

      quī vīdit mare turbidum et

NOTES AND VOCABULARY

Line 9:   **illī:** refers to the inventor of the first ship (*quī ... commīsit pelagō ratem ... prīmus*); dative of possession + *erat*: "there was to him," so "he had ..."; note that Horace often uses a singular verb with a plural subject; the verb agrees with the nearer singular subject.

          rōbur, rōburis, n. oak tree, oak wood; strength. Note that unlike most words for trees in Latin which are feminine, *rōbur* is neuter.

          aes, aeris, n. bronze. Don't confuse *aes* with *āēr, āeris,* n. "air."

          triplex, triplicis triple, i.e., very strong

Line 10: **circā,** *prep.* + *acc.* around

          pectus, pectoris, n. chest, heart. A word that looks very similar to *pectus* is *pecus, pecoris,* n. "flock."

          fragilis, fragile easily destroyed, fragile

          trux, trucis savage, cruel. Synonyms of *trux* include *saevus, -a, -um* and *crūdēlis, crūdēle.*

Line 11: **committō, committere, commīsī, commissum** to commit, entrust

          pelagus, -ī, n. sea; note the CHIASMUS in *fragilem trucī ... pelagō ratem.* Remember that there are many words in Latin that denote the sea: *mare, pontus, aequor, fretum* and by SYNECDOCHE *fluctus* and *unda.*

          ratis, ratis, f. raft; boat

Line 12: **prīmus:** i.e., he was the first one to do so

          praeceps, praecipitis rushing, headlong

          Āfricus, -ī, m. the southwest wind

Line 13:	**dēcertō** (1) (+ *dat.*) to contend with
	Aquilō, Aquilōnis, m. north wind, northeast wind, north-by-northeast wind; note that the syllable "qui-" of *Aquilō* scans short.
Line 14:	**trīstīs** = *trīstēs* sad, gloomy; the Hyades are said to have died while mourning the death of their brother Hyas. Transformed into a constellation, they could also be called "sad" because the rainy season prevailed during their rising and setting.
	Hyadēs, -um, f. the Hyades, a cluster of five stars in the constellation Taurus. Note that their name is borrowed from the Greek language, and so the Greek accusative form of the name is used: "*Hyadas*" instead of "*Hyadēs*."
	rabiēs, rabieī, f. madness; fury
	Notus, -ī, m. south wind
Line 15:	**quō:** the antecedent is *Notī;* ablative of comparison with *māior.* Translate "than which."
	arbiter, arbitrī, m.: here, "one who decides," thus: "judge" or "master." Supply the verb *est.* It is the wind that decides whether the sea can be crossed.
	Hadria, -ae, f. the Adriatic Sea
Line 16:	**tollō, tollere, sustulī, sublātum** to raise up, excite
	seu: This conjunction introduces an indirect question, and it should be noted that the first *seu* (before *tollere*) is understood. Translate "whether he wishes to . . . or to . . . ." The indirect question is dependent upon the decision process implied in the noun *arbiter.*
	pōnō, pōnere, posuī, positum to put (down), lay aside; to make quiet
	volt: archaic form of *vult.*
	fretum, -ī, n. strait; (in pl.) the sea
Line 17:	**quem + gradum:** Translate "what approach . . .?" "What approach of death" means "What [sort of] approaching death."
Line 18:	**quī:** The antecedent is the subject of *timuit;* again, the reference is to the inventor of the first ship. Note the ANAPHORA.
	siccus, -a, -um dry; *siccīs oculīs* means "without weeping."
	mōnstra natantia: supply *vīdit* from line 19; ANAPHORA often is accompanied by ELLIPSIS. *Mōnstra natantia* refer to creatures like whales, sharks, squids, etc., that inhabit the deep.
Line 19:	**turbidus, -a, -um** turbulent

HORACE *ODES* 1.3, CONTINUED

20   īnfāmīs scopulōs Ācroceraunia?

    nēquīquam deus abscidit

prūdēns ōceanō dissociābilī

    terrās, sī tamen impiae

nōn tangenda ratēs trānsiliunt vada.

25   audāx omnia perpetī

gēns hūmana ruit per vetitum nefās.

    audāx Īapetī genus

ignem fraude malā gentibus intulit.

    post ignem aetheriā domō

30   subductum maciēs et nova febrium

    terrīs incubuit cohors

sēmōtīque prius tarda necessitās

    lētī corripuit gradum.

NOTES AND VOCABULARY

Line 20:   **īnfāmīs** = *īnfāmēs*; note the accusative poetic plural ending.

        Ācroceraunia, -ōrum, n.: a very dangerous rocky promontory on the coast of Epirus that runs out into the Ionian Sea: Here, *Ācroceraunia* is in apposition to *īnfāmīs scopulōs*; translate "the notorious crags of Acroceraunia."

Line 21:   **nēquīquam,** *adv.* in vain

        abscindō, abscindere, abscidī, abscissum to tear away, cut off, separate

Line 22:   **prūdēns, prudentis** wise; i.e., "in his wisdom/providence"

        ōceanō: ablative of separation or means; here, *ōceanus* is equivalent to *mare.*

        dissociābilis, dissociābile incompatible

Line 23:   **sī tamen,** *conj.* if indeed

        impius, -a, -um irreverent; note the SYNCHESIS.

Line 24:   **nōn tangenda:** "which ought not be touched"

        trānsiliō, trānsilīre to leap across, hasten through

        vadum, -ī, n. ford; (in pl.) the sea

Line 25:   **audāx, audācis** (over)bold

omnia: direct object of *perpetī*

perpetior, perpetī, perpessus sum to tolerate, dare. This is what is called an "epexegetic" or explanatory infinitive. An epexegetic infinitive explains and further limits an adjective, in this case *audāx*; translate "overbold to dare."

Line 26:   **ruō, ruere, ruī** to rush

vetō, vetāre, vetuī, vetitum to deny, forbid

nefās (indeclinable) wickedness, something forbidden by or hateful to the gods; by extension, a monstrous or horrible thing

Line 27:   **Īapetus, -ī,** m. the Titan Iapetus. There is no myth attached to him other than his identification as the father of Prometheus, who created the human race and then stole fire from heaven for his creation. It was Prometheus's gift of fire that made human civilization possible.

genus, generis, n. progeny; here, translate "son." Other words in Latin for "son" include *fīlius* and *nātus.*

Line 28:   **fraus, fraudis,** f. theft

īnferō, īnferre, intulī, illātum to bring into, introduce

Line 29:   **aetherius, -a, -um** heavenly

domō: ablative of separation; translate "from its heavenly home."

Line 30:   **subdūcō, -ere, subdūxī, subductum** to steal, hide; translate *post ignem ... subductum* "after fire having been stolen," hence, "after the theft of fire." Note the CHIASMUS.

maciēs, maciēī, f. leanness, wasting disease

febris, febris, f. fever, disease; in order to offset the benefits of Prometheus's gift of fire to humankind, Jupiter gave the jar (or box) filled with evils to Pandora, which she opened.

Line 31:   **incumbō, incumbere, incubuī, incubitum** (+ *dat.*) to oppress, settle, weigh upon

cohors, cohortis, f. throng, cohort, crowd

Line 32:   **sēmōtus, -a, -um** removed, distant; note the CHIASMUS.

prius tarda: translate "slow in former times."

Lines 32–33:   **necessitās lētī:** "the necessity of death"; i.e., the fact that we die.

Line 33:   **corripiō, corripere, corripuī, correptum** to seize; hasten

gradus, gradūs, m. step, pace

HORACE *ODES* 1.3, CONTINUED

  expertus vacuum Daedalus āera

35   pinnīs nōn hominī datīs:

  perrūpīt Acheronta Herculeus labor.

   nīl mortālibus arduī est:

  caelum ipsum petimus stultitiā neque

   per nostrum patimur scelus

40 īrācunda Iovem pōnere fulmina.

NOTES AND VOCABULARY

Line 34: **experior, experīrī, expertus sum** to make a trial of, try out; to know
   from experience; supply *est* with *expertus*: "Daedalus tried . . . ."

   vacuus, -a, -um empty

   Daedalus, -ī, m. The mythical inventor who built the labyrinth that
   imprisoned the Minotaur. Daedalus was imprisoned by King Minos
   on the island of Crete after Theseus slew the Minotaur and escaped
   from the labyrinth. Daedalus then escaped from the island with his
   son Icarus by fashioning waxen wings that they used to fly away.

   āēr, āeris, m. air; again, note the Greek accusative.

Line 35: **pinna, -ae,** f. wing; ablative of means

   dō, dare, dedī, datum to allow, give

Line 36: **perrumpō, perrumpere, perrūpī, perruptum** to break through; the
   syllable "-it" is long here for the sake of the meter.

   Acherōn, Acherontis/Acherontos, m. Translate "the Underworld."
   A mythical river or lake that separates the world of the living from
   the world of the dead, often identified with the river Styx. Note that
   the name is a Greek loan word, and so the Greek third-declension
   accusative ending is used, *Acheronta* instead of *Acherontem*. Also,
   with regard to scansion, the "a" of Acheron is short because "ch"
   represents a single consonant, the Greek letter Chi.

   Herculeus, -a, -um of Hercules: The mythical hero Hercules had
   to perform 12 labors or tasks. His final labor was to enter the
   Underworld and bring the three-headed guard dog Cerberus back
   with him. Notice how Horace tracks human exploration from the
   top of the universe (heaven) to the bottom (the Underworld).

Line 37: **nīl,** n. nothing

   arduī: partitive genitive + *nīl*: translate "there is nothing [too]
   difficult."

Line 38: **petō, petere, petīvī, petītum** to seek, attempt, ask

stultitia, -ae, f. foolishness; *stultitiā* is an ablative of cause.

Line 39: **per,** *prep.* + *acc.* through, because of

patior, patī, passus sum to allow. Don't confuse *patior* with *pateō, patēre, patuī* "to lie open" or *partior, partīrī, partitus sum* "to divide."

scelus, sceleris, n. wickedness, crime

Line 40: **īrācunda:** This is a TRANSFERRED EPITHET: strictly speaking it is Jupiter who is angry, but grammatically the adjective modifies *fulmina*.

Iuppiter, Iovis, m. Jupiter, the king of the gods. His weapon is the thunderbolt. The idea is that Jupiter can never rest from punishing human arrogance and folly.

fulmen, fulminis, n. thunderbolt

COMPREHENSION QUESTIONS

1. Identify the addresse of this poem.

2. What does Horace pray that the addressee will be able to do?

3. What example does Horace give of mankind being overbold?

4. What example does Horace give of Prometheus being overbold? Cite the Latin.

5. What other two examples does Horace give of mythological individuals who were overbold?

READING 15

The virtuous lover requires no weapons wherever in the inhospitable world he may venture.

THE PURE-OF-HEART LOVER AND LALAGE

HORACE *ODES* 1.22

Meter: Sapphic

1   Integer vītae scelerisque pūrus

    nōn eget Maurīs iaculīs neque arcū,

    nec venēnātīs gravidā sagittīs,

        Fūsce, pharetrā,

5   sīve per Syrtīs iter aestuōsās

    sīve factūrus per inhospitālem

    Caucasum, vel quae loca fābulōsus

        lambit Hydaspēs.

NOTES AND VOCABULARY

Line 1:   **integer, integra, integrum** whole, untouched, upright

    vītae: genitive of reference, stating respect with which the adjective, *integer*, is applicable; in classical Latin an ablative of respect would be used more typically.

    scelus, sceleris, n. wrongdoing, crime, affliction; *sceleris* is a genitive of reference with *pūrus*.

    integer . . . pūrus: note the chiastic arrangement of the words.

Line 2:   **egeō, egēre, eguī** (+ *abl.*) to need, want

    Maurus, -a, -um Moorish, African

    iaculum, -ī, n. javelin

    arcus, arcūs, m. bow

Line 3:   **venēnātus, -a, -um** poisonous

    gravidus, -a, -um heavy, laden, weighed down

Line 4:   **Fūscus, -ī,** m. Aristius Fuscus was a literary friend of Horace, who is the addressee of one of his *Satires* and, later, one of his *Epistles*.

pharētra, -ae, f. quiver

Line 5:   **Syrtis, Syrtis,** f. Syrtis (especially plural), name of two areas of sandy flats on the coast between Carthage and Cyrene; the whole desert region lies next to this coast.

iter, itineris, n. journey

aestuōsus, -a, -um sweltering, very hot, agitated

Lines 5–6:   **sīve . . . sīve:** the form in which the catalog of places is presented recalls Catullus Poem 11, also in the Sapphic meter; the geographical catalog there also repeats the word *sīve* in enumerating alternatives.

Line 7:   **Caucasus, -ī,** m. Caucasus Mountains

quae loca: here, the antecedent (*loca*) is incorporated into the relative clause

fābulōsus, -a, -um legendary, storied; Horace may be responsible for coining the adjective *fābulōsus,* which makes its first appearance in Latin literature in this poem.

Line 8:   **lambō, lambere, lambī** to lick, wash

Hydaspēs, Hydaspis, m. Hydaspes, tributary of river Indus, which is located in India (modern Pakistan), the Jhelum.

HORACE *ODES* 1.22, CONTINUED

namque mē silvā lupus in Sabīnā,

10 dum meam cantō Lalagēn et ultrā

terminum cūrīs vagor expedītīs,

  fūgit inermem,

quāle portentum neque mīlitāris

Daunias lātīs alit aesculētīs,

15 nec Iubae tellūs generat, leōnum

  ārida nūtrīx.

pōne mē pigrīs ubi nūlla campīs

arbor aestīvā recreātur aurā,

quod latus mundī nebulae malusque

20 Iuppiter urget,

NOTES AND VOCABULARY

Lines 9–12: **mē . . . inermem:** note the HYPERBATON; *mē* is placed first in this sentence for emphasis.

Line 9: **silvā . . . in Sabīnā:** Horace's country home, his Sabine farm, was located in Sabine territory.

lupus, -ī, m. wolf; the arrangement of the words *silvā lupus in Sabīnā* places the wolf in the Sabine forest.

Line 10: **cantō** (1) to sing, sing about, recite

Lalagē, Lalagēs, f., Lalage, woman's name; Greek for "chatterer." In the accusative case singular, most Greek nouns in Latin end in –an, –on, –en, or –a. *Lalagen* in line 10 is such a Greek accusative.

ultrā, *prep.* + *acc.* beyond

Line 11: **terminus, -ī,** m. boundary line, limit

cūra, -ae, f. care, concern, worry, a person or thing constituting an object of care

vagor (1) to wander

expediō, expedīre, expedīvī, expedītum to free, extricate, release

| Line 12: | **fūgit:** perfect tense, not present, because the "u" is long |

inermis, inerme unarmed. When a prefix is added to a base that has a short "a" followed by two consonants, the vowel is changed to an "e." Thus *in + arm- = inermis, in* = "not" + *arm-* "armed."

| Line 13: | **portentum, -ī,** n. monster, portent, abnormal phenomenon |

quāle portentum: accusative, direct object of *alit* (14)

| Line 14: | **Daunias, Dauniadis,** f., Apulia, region of southeastern Italy; Daunus was a legendary king of Apulia; Horace comes from the town of Venusia on the border between Apulia and Lucania. |

alō, alere, aluī, altum to nourish

aesculētum, -ī, n. oak forest

| Line 15: | **Iuba, -ae,** m. Juba, Juba I, Numidian king who supported Pompey in the civil war |

tellūs, tellūris, f. land, earth, country, ground

generō (1) to produce, create

| Line 16: | **āridus, -a, -um** dry |

nūtrīx, nūtricis, f. nurse, especially a wet nurse; *ārida nūtrīx* is an example of OXYMORON.

| Line 17: | **pōne:** repeated as the first word of line 21; note the ANAPHORA. |

piger, pigra, pigrum lifeless, inactive, lazy

campus, -ī, m. plain, level surface; plain, field

| Line 18: | **aestīvus, -a, -um** summer |

recreō (1) to recreate, restore, revive

aura, -ae, f. breeze; remember to distinguish carefully between *aurum, -ī,* n. "gold" and *auris, auris,* f. "ear" and this noun, *aura, -ae.*

| Line 19: | **latus, lateris,** n. side, extreme part or region, flank, lungs, body; *quod latus mundī* is parallel to *ubi . . . aurā* (17–18); the antecedent, *latus (mundī),* is incorporated into the relative clause; cf. *quae loca* (7) above. Do not confuse *latus, lateris,* n. "side" (line 19) with *lātus, -a, -um* "wide, broad" (line 14) nor with the verb *lateo, latēre, latuī* "to lie hidden." |

mundus, -ī, m. world

nebula, -ae, f. cloud, mist, fog

| Line 20: | **Iuppiter:** (with *malus,* line 19) bad weather (by METONYMY) |

urget: agrees with the nearer noun, although it has a double subject, both *nebulae* and *Iuppiter.*

HORACE *ODES* 1.22, CONTINUED

pōne sub currū nimium propinquī

sōlis in terrā domibus negāta:

dulce rīdentem Lalagēn amābō,

   dulce loquentem.

NOTES AND VOCABULARY

Line 21:   **pōne:** understand *mē* again.

   currus, currūs, m. chariot. The chariot of the sun is driven across the sky each day by the god of the sun; the Tropics would represent the area where his chariot gets too near the earth.

   nimium, *adv.* too, too much, very

   propinquus, -a, -um near, neighboring; *propinquī* is genitive, modifying *sōlis* (line 22).

Line 22:   **sōl, sōlis,** m. sun; be careful not to confuse *sōl, sōlis* with *sōlus, -a, -um* "alone, only" or with *solum, -ī,* n. "soil, ground."

   domibus: dative with *negāta*

Line 23:   **dulce:** here, adverb; the positive degree of the adverb of *dulcis* has two forms: *dulciter* and *dulce. Dulce* also is the form of the neuter singular.

Lines 23–24:   These two lines echo both Catullus 51.5 (*dulce rīdentem* "sweetly laughing") and Sappho 31.3–5 ("sweetly speaking . . . and laughing in a lovely manner"). Note that Horace "reintroduces" Sappho's "sweetly speaking," which Catullus chooses not to follow in his adaptation of Sappho 31.

COMPREHENSION QUESTIONS

1.   What does the man upright in life and free from crime not need? Cite the Latin.

2.   What fled from Horace when he was in the Sabine forest?

3.   In what type of climate does Horace wish to be placed?

CHAPTER 6

PUBLIUS OVIDIUS NASO

AN INTRODUCTION TO OVID

By the time he was in his twenties, Ovid (Publius Ovidius Naso) had established himself as a successful poet in Rome. By the time he reached his fifties, he was at the pinnacle of his career and was the toast of the city. In 8 CE, however, disaster struck; the *princeps* Augustus exiled Ovid to Tomis, a bleak outpost on the Black Sea and as far from Rome as a truly urban Roman could get.

Ovid was born on March 20, 43 BCE into a wealthy equestrian family of Sulmo located in the central part of Italy to the east of Rome. His family wanted him to pursue a civil/military career but, instead, Ovid turned to the writing of poetry, and published his first poetic work, the five original books of the *Amōrēs,* by 20 BCE. This collection of poems was later revised and published in three books. Between these two editions Ovid published the *Herōidēs,* a series of letters from various heroic women to their husbands or lovers. He then turned to mock-didactic poems, works that purport to educate an audience, and published the *Medicāmina Facēī Fēmineae,* a work on women's cosmetics; the *Ars Amātōria,* a treatise on how to meet women in Rome; and the *Remēdia Amōris,* a sequel to the *Ars Amātōria* that deals with how to end a relationship.

All of these works contributed enormously to Ovid's popularity as a virtuoso poet and a writer who had his finger on the pulse of elite Rome. But it was his longer poems, the *Metamorphōsēs* and the *Fastī* (of which only six books survive), that have ensured his immortality. The *Metamorphōsēs* has become one of the most important literary sources for Greek and Roman mythology. In the poem Ovid brings together his erudition, his enormous wit, an intricate plan that incorporates, among other structures, the

Hellenistic design of tales within tales, and his inventive and easy to read poetic style. The work begins with the creation of the world and ends with the power and might of Rome.

Ovid was occupied with the writing and publication of these epics until 8 CE, when his life took an unexpected and tragic turn, and he was exiled by Augustus. Ovid supplies two reasons for his banishment, "a poem and a mistake" (*carmen et error*). The *carmen* probably refers to the *Ars Amātōria*, a poem published at least a decade before his exile, while the *error* remains unknown, although clearly it was the principal reason he was expelled from Italy.

Ovid continued to write in exile: his two works, the *Trīstia* and the *Epistulae ex Pontō*, combine descriptions of his journey and new life with entreaties for forgiveness and an end to his banishment. The death of Augustus in 14 CE raised his hopes that he might win over Augustus's successor Tiberius to allow his return to Rome. Ovid did not prevail, however, and he himself died three years later in exile in 17 CE.

Statue of Ovid. Constanța, the oldest city in Romania and known in ancient times as Tomis, is the place where Augustus exiled the poet Ovid who died here eight years later. (©Wikimedia Commons)

READING 16

The story of Daedalus and Icarus forms part of a larger story about King Minos of Crete told in Books 7–8 of the *Metamorphōsēs*. Daedalus with his son, Icarus, fled from Athens to Crete after he was condemned for murdering his nephew, Perdix (*Metamorphōsēs* 8.241–259). Daedalus, who was very well known for his skill in the arts, constructed the labyrinth to contain the Minotaur, a monster, half man, half bull, the offspring of an unnatural union between the king's wife, Pasiphae, and a bull. This maze was so complex that the artist himself could scarcely find his way out of it. Minos would not allow Daedalus to leave the island for fear he would reveal the secret of the labyrinth's passages. Although little is said of Daedalus's sojourn in Crete, the poet describes him as discontented with his lengthy exile there. To escape, he fashions wings from bird feathers and beeswax for himself and his son, with which they seek flight. Although Daedalus advises Icarus appropriately on the dangers of flying too high or too low, he disregards his father's advice by flying too close to the sun, which melts the waxen wings thereby causing him to plummet to his death into the sea.

The story illustrates an essential precept of Aristotelian philosophy, that man be moderate in all things. Icarus violates the law by flying too close to the sun; Daedalus, by attempting to change nature itself by constructing man-made wings for himself and his son.

Epitomizing so beautifully the nature of artistic creativity, this story has been a favorite topic for artists from antiquity until the present. As the epigram to his novel *The Portrait of an Artist as a Young Man*, James Joyce chose from this story the words *ignōtās animum dīmittit in artēs* (line 188), and he named the hero of his story Stephen Dedalus. Ovid's myth has provided inspiration for numerous other writers, including Baudelaire, W. H. Auden, and Mallermé, and has been a favorite subject for artists such as Bruegel, Rubens, Tintoretto, Picasso, and Chagall.

The Lament for Icarus, Herbert James Draper (1863–1920). This painting portrays Icarus surrounded by grieving nymphs after his failed attempt at flight. (©Wiki-media Commons)

THE ESCAPE OF DAEDALUS AND ICARUS FROM CRETE

OVID *METAMORPHŌSĒS* 8.183–235

Meter: Dactylic Hexameter

> Daedalus intereā Crētēn longumque perōsus
> exilium tāctusque locī nātālis amōre
> 185 clausus erat pelagō. "terrās licet" inquit "et undās
> obstruat: at caelum certē patet; ībimus illāc:
> omnia possideat, nōn possidet āera Mīnōs."
> dīxit et ignōtās animum dīmittit in artēs
> nātūramque novat. nam pōnit in ōrdine pennās
> 190 ā minimā coeptās, longam breviōre sequentī,
> ut clīvō crēvisse putēs: sīc rūstica quondam

NOTES AND VOCABULARY

Line 183: **Crētē, Crētēs,** f. Crete, an island in the eastern Mediterranean Sea. *Crētēn* is a Greek accusative singular, direct object of *perōsus*.

perōdī, perōdisse, perōsum to despise, loathe. This verb has lost its present tense forms; therefore, its perfect forms carry present meaning. The perfect passive participle should be translated actively as "hating, loathing."

Line 184: **nātālis, nātāle** of birth; *locī nātālis*: Daedalus was an Athenian by birth.

Line 185: **licet:** here, used as a conjunction meaning "although." It introduces a subjunctive clause with *obstruat*, with Minos as an implied subject.

Line 186: **obstruō, obstruere obstruxī, obstructum** to block, close

at, *conj.* but, yet; don't confuse the two conjunctions *at* and *ac*. *At* means "but"; *ac* means "and."

pateō, patēre, patuī to be open, accessible

illāc: by that way

Line 187: **possideat:** a concessive subjunctive used in an independent sentence; translate "even though he may possess." Sentences with a concessive subjunctive are introduced in English by "though," "even though," or "granted that." The verb occurs in two tenses of the subjunctive only, present for present time and perfect for past time. The negative is *nē*.

āēr, āeris, m., air; *āera* is a Greek accusative singular.

Mīnōs, Mīnōis, m. Minos, king of Crete, husband to Pasiphae, father of Ariadne, and the one who ordered the labyrinth built.

Line 188: **ignōtus, -a, -um** unknown; here suggesting previously unknown

dīmittō, dīmittere, dīmīsī, dīmissum to let go, send away

Line 189: **novō** (1) to make new, change; *nātūramque novat* begins the description of the man-made metamorphosis.

ōrdō, ōrdinis, m. row, order, position

penna, -ae, f. feather

Line 190: **coepī, coepisse, coeptum** to have begun. Like *perōdī* (line 183 above), *coepī* has lost its present voice system and thus is called a defective verb. Unlike the forms of *perōdī*, which have a present meaning ("I hate"), however, those of *coepī* carry the past or perfect meaning ("I began" or "I have begun"). The present tense is supplied by *incipiō*. Some critics believe that Ovid did not compose line 190—that is, the line is a later addition to the text—for two reasons. First, the description in line 190, "the shorter feather following the long [feather]," contradicts the thought in the result clause in line 191, [the feathers were organized] "so that you would think they had grown on a hillside" (taller trees on top, shorter on the bottom) as well as the comparison of the ordering of the feathers to that of reeds of a panpipe in line 192. In addition, the –i ending of *sequentī* is problematical, for participles ending in –i function as adjectives, as in line 197 (*ore renīdentī*). Some critics who do not construe the line as an interpolation emend *sequentī* to *sequente*.

Line 191: **ut:** introduces a result clause without the expected *tam* or *tālis*.

clīvus, -ī, m. slope, incline; *clīvō* is an ablative of place with the omission of the preposition *in*.

crēscō, crēscere, crēvī, crētum to grow, arise; *crēvisse* is a perfect active infinitive in an indirect statement with the understood accusative subject being *pennās*.

putō (1) to think

sīc: introduces a SIMILE.

OVID *METAMORPHŌSĒS* 8.183–235, CONTINUED

fistula disparibus paulātim surgit avēnīs;

tum līnō mediās et cērīs alligat īmās

atque ita conpositās parvō curvāmine flectit,

195 ut vēras imitētur avēs. puer Īcarus ūnā

stābat et, ignārus sua sē tractāre perīcla,

ōre renīdentī modo, quās vaga mōverat aura,

captābat plūmās, flāvam modo pollice cēram

mollībat lūsūque suō mīrābile patris

200 impediēbat opus. postquam manus ultima coeptō

inposita est, geminās opifex lībrāvit in ālās

ipse suum corpus mōtāque pependit in aurā;

instruit et nātum "mediō" que "ut līmite currās,

NOTES AND VOCABULARY

Line 192: **fistula, -ae,** f. pipe, panpipe

dispār, disparis unequal, dissimilar

paulātim, *adv.* gradually, little by little

surgō, surgere, surrēxī, surrēctum to rise

avēna, -ae, f. stem, stalk

Line 193: **līnum, -ī,** n. thread, string—probably made from the flax plant.

cēra, -ae, f. wax

alligō (1) to tie, fasten

īmus, -a, -um lowest, bottom; note the SYNCHESIS in *līnō mediās cērīs īmās,* which literally binds the line together just as the string binds the feathers together.

Line 194: **conpōnō, conpōnere, conposuī, conpositum** to join, place together

curvāmen, curvāminis, n. curvature, arc

flectō, flectere, flexī, flextum to bend, twist

Line 195: **imitor** (1) to imitate

Īcarus, -ī, m. Icarus, Daedalus's son.

ūnā, *adv.* at the same time; don't forget to distinguish between *ūnā, adv.* "at the same time" and *ūnus, -a, -um* "one."

Line 196: **ignārus, -a, -um** unaware

tractō (1) to handle, manage

perīcla: a syncopated form of *perīcula*; "dangers"; i.e., that which will endanger Icarus's life. *sua sē tractāre perīcla* is an indirect statement dependent on *ignārus*.

Line 197:   **renīdeō, renīdēre** to smile with pleasure, beam

    modo . . . modo, *adv.* now . . . now, at one time . . . at another; these correlatives lend an immediacy and visual element to the narrative.

    vagus, -a, -um shifting, moving about

Line 198:   **captō** (1) to try to catch. *Captō* belongs to a group of verbs that derive from the fourth principle part of another verb. These verbs, formed from the root of the first supine, end in –to, –ito, or –so. Because they convey the notion of force or repetition, they are referred to as intensives or frequentatives or iteratives. Other examples besides *captō*, meaning "to try to catch," from *capiō, capere, cēpī, captum,* include *pulsō*, "to beat repeatedly, pulsate" from *pellō, pellere, pulsī, pulsum,* and *iactō*, "to throw with force, hurl," from *iaciō, iacere, iēcī, iactum.*

    plūma, -ae, f. feather

    flāvus, -a, -um yellow

    pollex, pollicis, m. thumb

Line 199:   **molliō, mollīre, mollīvī, mollitum** to soften, weaken; *mollībat =* *molliēbat.*

    lūsus, lūsūs, m. play, sport

    mīrābilis, -e wonderful, wondrous

Line 200:   **impediō, impedīre, impedīvī, impedītum** to hinder, impede

    manus ultima: i.e., the finishing touch

    coeptum, -ī, n. design, undertaking; *coeptō* is dative case because of the compound verb *inponō.*

Line 201:   **opifex, opificis,** m. craftsman, artisan

    lībrō (1) to level, balance

Line 202:   **mōtā . . . in aurā:** i.e., air moved by the beating of the wings.

    pendeō, pendēre, pependī to hang

Line 203:   **instruō, instruere, instruxī, instructum** to equip, provide

    medius, -a, -um middle; the essence of Daedalus's speech (203–204) to his son is found in this first word of fatherly advice. The conjunction *et* is postponed from the first place in the sentence to the second place. A freestanding *-que* such as in the middle of *"mediō"que . . . ait* is not often seen in Latin. Translate as though *-que* were attached to *ait.*

    līmes, līmitis, m. path, road, course

OVID *METAMORPHŌSĒS* 8.183–235, CONTINUED

Īcare," ait "moneō, nē, sī dēmissior ībis,

205 unda gravet pennās, sī celsior, ignis adūrat:

inter utrumque volā. nec tē spectāre Boōtēn

aut Helicēn iubeō strictumque Ōrīonis ēnsem:

mē duce carpe viam!" pariter praecepta volandī

trādit et ignōtās umerīs accommodat ālās.

210 inter opus monitūsque genae maduēre senīlēs,

et patriae tremuēre manūs; dedit ōscula nātō

nōn iterum repetenda suō pennīsque levātus

ante volat comitīque timet, velut āles, ab altō

quae teneram prōlem prōdūxit in āera nīdō,

215 hortāturque sequī damnōsāsque ērudit artēs

et movet ipse suās et nātī respicit ālās.

NOTES AND VOCABULARY

Line 204: **nē:** introduces two negative purpose clauses (*gravet* and *adūrat*) with ASYNDETON.

dēmissus, -a, -um low, close to the ground

Line 205: **gravō** (1) to weigh down

celsus, -a, -um high, lofty

ignis, ignis, m. fire, heat of the sun

adūrō, adūere, adussī, adustum to burn, scorch

Line 206: **volō** (1) to fly; be careful to distinguish *volō, volāre* "to fly" from *volō, velle* "to wish."

Boōtēs, -ae, m. a bright constellation in the North, next to the Great Bear (Ursa Major) constellation. *Boōtēn* is a Greek accusative case used as the direct object of *spectāre*.

Line 207: **Helicē, Helicēs,** f. the Greek name for the constellation Ursa Major. *Helicēn* is another Greek accusative, here the direct object of *spectāre*, line 206. The name comes from *helix*, "rolling" or "twisting," since the constellation spins around the north star and never sets below the horizon.

stringō, stringere, strinxī, strictum to unsheathe, draw

Ōrīōn, Ōrīonis, m. the constellation in the South known as the Hunter. Its rising and setting are often associated with storms.

Line 208:	**pariter,** *adv.* at the same time, together
	praeceptum, -ī, n. lesson, command, instruction
Line 209:	**trādō, trādere, trādidī, trāditum** to hand down, deliver

ignōtās: perhaps meant to recall line 188 and *ignārus* of line 196. The adjective foreshadows the tragedy about to beset Icarus.

accommodō (1) (+ *dat.*) to adjust, apply

āla, -ae, f. wing

Line 210: **monitus, monitūs,** m. warning, admonition

gena, -ae, f. cheek

madeō, madēre, maduī to grow wet; *maduēre* and *tremuēre* (in line 211) are the syncopated forms of the third person plural perfect *maduērunt* and *tremuērunt*.

senīlis, senīle old, aged

Line 211: **patrius, -a, -um** of a father, paternal

Line 212: **repetō, repetere, repetīvī, repetītum** to return; translate *repetenda* "to be returned."

suō: the separation of the adjective from its noun, HYPERBATON, heightens the pathos of the scene.

levō (1) to raise up, lift

Line 213: **ante,** *adv.* in front, before

comes, comitis, m. partner, companion; *comitīque* is a dative of reference indicating for whom Daedalus was concerned.

āles, ālitis, m./f. bird. The common word for bird is *avis, avis,* f./m. The word *āles, ālitis,* m./f. is derived from *āla, -ae,* f., "wing," and thus *āles,* literally meaning the "winged one," also has the definition of "bird."

Line 214: **tener, tenera, tenerum** tender, sensitive, fragile

prōlēs, prōlis, f. child, offspring

nīdus, -ī, m. nest. The exaggerated separation of the noun from its adjective, HYPERBATON, creates suspense and interest until the SIMILE is resolved. The placement of *nīdō* next to *āera* intensifies the height of the nest.

Line 215: **hortor** (1) to urge, encourage

damnōsus, -a, -um destructive, ruinous

ērudiō, ērudīre, ērudīvī, ērudītum to teach, instruct

Line 216: **respiciō, respicere, respexī, respectum** to look at, look back at

OVID *METAMORPHŌSĒS* 8.183–235, CONTINUED

> hōs aliquis tremulā dum captat harundine piscēs,
>
> aut pāstor baculō stīvāve innīxus arātor
>
> vīdit et obstipuit, quīque aethera carpere possent,
>
> 220   crēdidit esse deōs. et iam Iūnōnia laevā
>
> parte Samos (fuerant Dēlosque Parosque relictae)
>
> dextra Lebinthos erat fēcundaque melle Calymnē,
>
> cum puer audācī coepit gaudēre volātū
>
> dēseruitque ducem caelīque cupīdine tractus
>
> 225   altius ēgit iter. rapidī vīcīnia sōlis
>
> mollit odōrātas, pennārum vincula, cērās;
>
> tābuerant cērae: nūdōs quatit ille lacertōs,

NOTES AND VOCABULARY

Line 217:   **hōs:** "them" (i.e., Daedalus and Icarus) is the object of *vīdit, obstipuit,* and *crēdidit;* the pronoun occurs at the start of the sentence for emphasis. Note that verbs are appropriately singular with subjects *aliquis . . . aut pāstor . . . arātor.*

              tremulus, -a, -um trembling, quivering

              harundō, harundinis, f. a reed, sharpened reed, arrow; here, a rod for fishing

Line 218:   **pāstor, pāstōris,** m. shepherd

              baculum, -ī, n. walking stick, staff

              stīva, -ae, f. the shaft of a plow handle

              innītor, innītī, innīxus sum (+ *abl.*) to lean on, rest on; take *innīxus* with both *pāstor* and *arātor.*

              arātor, arātōris, m. a plowman

Line 219:   **obstipescō, obstipescere, obstipuī** to be amazed, astonished

              aethēr, aetheris, m. sky, air; *āēr, āeris,* m. "air" and *aethēr, aetheris,* m. "air" are synonyms.

              possent: subjunctive in a relative clause of characteristic explaining why Daedalus and Icarus are believed to be gods.

Line 220:   **Iūnōnius, -a, -um** of or pertaining to Juno

              laevus, -a, -um left, left hand; *laevā parte* is an ablative of place with the omission of the preposition *in.*

| Line 221: | **Samos, -ī,** f. an island in the eastern Mediterranean off the coast of Asia Minor between Ephesus and Miletus. Its temple to Juno, built in the sixth century BCE, was the largest in the Greek world at the time. |

Samos, -ī, f. an island in the eastern Mediterranean off the coast of Asia Minor between Ephesus and Miletus. Its temple to Juno, built in the sixth century BCE, was the largest in the Greek world at the time.

Dēlos, -ī, f. a small (two square miles) island in the Aegean revered as the birthplace of Apollo and Diana.

Paros, -ī, f. another island in the Aegean most known for its fine white marble and as the birthplace of the seventh-century Greek poet Archilochus.

Line 222: **Lebinthos, -ī,** f. an island in the Sporadic chain, off the east coast of mainland Greece. Note that *dextra* is nominative case, modifying *Lebinthos*; translate, however, "on the right side."

erat: although singular, the verb has Samos, Lebinthos, and Calymne as its subjects.

fēcundus, -a, -um fertile, fruitful

mel, mellis, n. honey

Calymnē, -ēs, f. an island off the coast of Asia Minor near Rhodes. It is known for its honey. Note the Greek ending.

Line 223: **gaudeō, gaudēre, gāvīsus sum** (+ *abl.*) to rejoice in

volātus, volātūs, m. flying, flight. Note how the fourth principal part of *volō, volāre, volāvī, volātum* becomes the fourth declension noun, *volātus, volātūs,* m. a "flight" (line 223). Likewise the fourth principal part of *lūdō, lūdere, lūdī, lūsum* becomes the noun *lūsus, lūsūs,* m. "play, playing" (line 199), and the fourth part of *moneō, monēre, monuī, monitum* becomes the noun *monitus, monitūs,* m. "admonition" (line 210).

Line 224: **dēserō, dēsere, dēseruī, dēsertum** to abandon, desert

cupīdō, cupīdinis, m. desire, eagerness

Line 225: **agō, agere, ēgī, āctum** to drive, do; *ēgit iter* refers to his flying.

rapidus, -a, -um scorching, fierce

vīcīnia, -ae, f. nearness, proximity

Line 226: **mollit:** reminiscent of the young boy mischievously softening the wax with the warmth of his own thumb (line 199). Now the sun softens the wax.

odōrātus, -a, -um fragrant, scented

Line 227: **tābescō, tābescere, tābuī** to melt gradually

quatiō, quatere, quassī, quassum to shake, move

lacertus, -ī, m. arm

OVID *METAMORPHŌSĒS* 8.183–235, CONTINUED

> rēmigiōque carēns nōn ūllās percipit aurās,
>
> ōraque caeruleā patrium clāmantia nōmen
>
> 230 excipiuntur aquā, quae nōmen trāxit ab illō.
>
> at pater īnfēlīx, nec iam pater, "Īcare," dīxit,
>
> "Īcare," dīxit "ubi es? quā tē regiōne requīram?"
>
> "Īcare," dīcēbat: pennās aspexit in undīs
>
> dēvōvitque suās artēs corpusque sepulcrō
>
> 235 condidit, et tellūs ā nōmine dicta sepultī.

NOTES AND VOCABULARY

Line 228:   **rēmigium, -(i)ī,** n. oars, wings. Note the various ways that Ovid expresses the idea of wings. *Āla, -ae,* f. is the ordinary Latin word for "wing." *Penna, -ae,* f. comes to mean "wing" through its meaning "feather," while *rēmigium, -(i)ī,* n.—"the oars of a boat"—is used in poetry, through association, to mean "wings."

   percipiō, percipere, percēpī, perceptum to catch, secure

Line 229:   **caeruleus, -a, -um** blue, greenish blue. HYPERBATON separates this adjective from its noun in the next line. This tightly constructed phrase (*oraque . . . aquā*) consists of a CHIASMUS entwined with a double SYNCHESIS, perhaps to reflect the contorted spiraling fall of Icarus from the sky.

Line 230:   **excipiō, excipere, excēpī, exceptum** to accept, receive

   quae: the antecedent is *aquā,* the body of water known as the Icarian Sea.

Line 231:   **nec iam,** *adv.* and no longer

Line 232:   **requīrō, requīrere, requīsīvī, requīsītum** to look for, ask for; *requīram* is a deliberative subjunctive. Translate "am I to seek" or "should I seek." The deliberative subjunctive is used in questions or exclamations to express doubt, indignation, or the impossibility of something's being done. This subjunctive uses the present tense for present time and the imperfect tense for past time. These questions often are RHETORICAL QUESTIONS and do not expect an answer. The negative is *nōn.*

Line 234:   **dēvoveō, dēvovēre, dēvōvī, devōtum** to curse

   sepulcrum, -ī, n. grave, tomb

Line 235:   **condō, condere, condidī, conditum** to found, establish, put away,
              store

              tellūs, tellūris, f. land; this is the island Icaria near Samos. Once again
              Ovid ends his tale with a reference to an aition (origin). This word is
              a synonym of *terrae, -ae,* f., a word seen in line 185. Both the Icarian
              Sea and the island Icaria are named after Icarus and are examples of
              eponymous myths. Such a myth explains how something received
              its name.

              sepeliō, sepelīre, sepelīvī, sepultum to bury. Here, genitive singular
              with *nōmine,* and referring to the boy, Icarus.

COMPREHENSION QUESTIONS

1. Give the three reasons supplied in lines 183–185 that Daedalus
   wants to leave Crete. Cite the Latin.

2. While his father is creating wings, what is Icarus doing? Cite the
   Latin.

3. What instructions does Daedalus give Icarus?

4. Who sees Daedalus and Icarus as they fly from Crete?

5. What happens after Daedalus and Icarus pass Lebinthus and
   Clymene?

6. How does Daedalus react when he spots Icarus's wings?

CHAPTER 7

POST-ANTIQUE LATIN WRITERS

AN INTRODUCTION TO POST-ANTIQUE LATIN WRITERS

The amount of surviving Latin literature written in Europe after the collapse of the Western Roman Empire in the late fifth century CE is larger than the surviving corpus of literature left by the Romans themseves. The very pulse of western European civilization moved primarily to the rhythms of Latin prose and poetry. The language of Caesar and Cicero performed new functions as Latin became the vehicle for the sciences, cartography, geography, history, and ethnography. But medieval, Renaissance, and Baroque Latin was not merely the language of scholars, scientists, and philosophers; it also produced poetry, letters, satire, fiction, and many other genres—including works widely recognized as masterpieces of world literature, such as Thomas More's *Utopia* and Erasmus's *Praise of Folly*. Even as the language of creative literature, Latin still rivaled the vernacular tongues in the Renaissance and Baroque period.

This international and multicultural role of Latin was in some ways already anticipated as people from the Western provinces began using Latin and not their native tongues as a means of expression. Latin's multicultural role was even more pronounced in the Middle Ages, Renaissance, and Baroque period when Latin served as an international language and a vehicle for a literary tradition eventually extending even to the New World. Men of letters from this period often wrote and spoke to one another in Latin. Thus their thoughts and style of writing were influenced by one another, while they were also influenced by the texts from antiquity.

This section illuminates this bounty of Latin, presenting two poems from the Baroque period. The passages reveal the enduring influence of the Roman poet Horace on the writings and thoughts of later generations.

READING 17

Lieven De Meyere (1655–1730) was born in Ghent, Flanders, and entered the Jesuits, an order of Catholic priests, at the customary age in those days of eighteen. He proved a brilliant student and enjoyed a long teaching career. He spent most of his career at the Jesuit College at Louvain, which was established in 1621. De Meyere taught humanities, philosophy, scripture, moral theology, and scholastic theology. He served eight years as dean of the college and two separate terms as an administrator for his religious community.

De Meyere published various treatises on theology as well as several volumes of poetry, which culminated in a 1727 edition in twelve books. For his handbook *De institutione principis libri III* (*On the Training of the Prince*), De Meyere used dactylic hexameter.

Considered one of the best Neo-Latin poets from Flanders and the southern Netherlands, he modeled himself on the Roman poet Propertius and strove for classical perfection in both form and diction. In this poem De Meyere pays homage to Horace and reveals his thorough knowledge of his predecessor's works.

IN PRAISE OF HORACE

LIEVEN DE MEYERE *LIBER* 1, *ODE* 6

Meter: Unusual tristich stanzas, consisting of (1) a dactylic hexameter; (2) an iambic dimeter; and (3) a dactylic catalectic trimester.

Horātiī Prīncipis Lyricōrum Laudēs

1   Flacce, lyrā cantūque potēns haerentia vīvis
          Movēre saxa rūpibus,
          Thrēiciumque nemus

     Carmine nātīvīs trādūcere montibus, ut quī
5   Acheronta rūpit Orpheus;
          Thrācia quem Rhodopē

NOTES AND VOCABULARY

Title: **prīnceps, prīncipis,** m. most eminent, chief, prince

               laus, laudis, f. praise

Line 1:   **Flacce:** vocative of Flaccus, the cognomen of Quintus Horatius Flaccus, the Roman poet Horace

               lyrā cantūque: ablative of respect with *potēns*

               cantus, cantūs, m. song

               haereō, haerēre, haesī, haesum (+ *dat.*) to cling to

Lines 1–2: Note the SYNCHESIS.

Line 2:   **movēre:** epexegetic infinitive dependent on *potēns*

               rūpes, rupis, f. cliff

Line 3:   **Thrēicius, -a, -um** Thracian. Thrace is the land of Orpheus, the legendary musician who went down to Hades to rescue his wife Eurydice and whose song "drew iron tears down Pluto's cheek" (John Milton, "Il Penseroso," line 107). The power of Orpheus's song moved stones and tree and tamed the savage beast. Poets looked to Orpheus as a poetic ancestor and source of inspiration.

               nemus, nemoris, n. wood, forest, grove

Line 4:   **carmen, carminis,** n. song, poem

               nātīvīs ... montibus: ablative of place from which

               trādūcō, trādūcere, trādūxī, trāductum to transfer, bring across, lead over

               ut quī, *conj.* translate "in the same way as."

Line 5:   **Acheron, Acherontis,** m. the river of woe in Hades

               rumpō, rumpere, rūpī, ruptum to break, tear

               Acheronta rūpit: translate "broke (the bonds of) the Acheron" (when he went to the Underworld to rescue Eurydice).

Line 6:   **Rhodopē, Rhodopēs,** f. a mountain range in Thrace

Lines 6–7: **Thrācia ... ferārum:** translate "at whom softening (taming) the spirit of the wild beasts Thracian Rhodope once marveled."

Ōlim admirāta est animōs mollīre ferārum,

    Tū Pindarō potentior

    Carmen ad Ausoniōs

10 Dēdūcis numerōs variā testūdine vātēs:

    Ut nūper āles Daulias

    Caedem Itylī memorāns,

Omnia Daedaleō discrīmina gutture vōcum

    Prīnceps recēnset ālitum:

15   Sīc lyra pulsa manū

Nīl humile aut ēnerve sonat; sublīmis et audāx

    Vexāre cantū sīdera.

    Sīve agitās vitium

NOTES AND VOCABULARY

Line 7:   **admiror** (1) to admire, respect, be surprised (at), be astonished (at)

Line 8:   **Pindarus, -ī,** m. Pindar, the Greek lyric poet; *Pindarō*: ablative of comparison

Line 9:   Note the allusion here to *Odes* 3.30.

    Ausōnius, -a, -um Italian; the Ausones were an indigenous people of central Italy.

Line 10:   **dēdūcō, dēdūcere, dēdūxī, dēductum** to adapt

    numerus, -ī, m. rhythm, meter (by METONYMY)

    testūdō, testūdinis, f. shell of a tortoise; lyre (by SYNECDOCHE); ablative of description; translate "a poet with a varied lyre."

    vātēs, vātis, m./f. bard, poet; appositive to the subject of *dēdūcis*

Line 11:   **ut:** translate "as"; the comparison is completed in the *sīc* clause below, lines 15ff.

    nūper, *adv.* not long ago, lately, recently

    āles, ālitis, m./f. bird; *āles* refers to Procne.

    Daulias, Dauliadis Daulian; Daulis was a town in central Greece noted for the story of Procne and Philomela.

Line 12:	**Itylus, -ī,** m. Itylus; Itylus, the son of Zethus, king of Thebes, was accidentally killed by his mother Aedon. He is here confused with Itys, the son of Procne. The Daulian bird is Procne, the mother of Itys whom she killed and served as a meal to her husband Tereus for his violating her sister Philomela. Tereus pursues them, but they are all changed into birds: Tereus into a hoopoe and Procne and Philomela into a nightingale and swallow, or vice versa. According to tradition, the gods took pity on Aedon in her grief, and she, too was turned into a nightingale.
Line 13:	**discrīmen, discrīminis,** n. distinction, difference
	Daedaleō ... gutture: ablative of means; translate "by means of a Daedalian throat."
	guttur, gutteris, n. throat; note the SYNCHESIS.
	vōcum: this genitive should be taken with *discrīmina*.
Line 14:	**prīnceps:** translate "most eminent."
	prīnceps ... ālitum: modifies *āles* (line 11).
	recēnseō, recēnsēre, recēnsuī, recēnsum to count, review
Line 15:	**Sīc:** introduces the other half of the comparison begun with *ut* in line 11.
	pellō, pellere, pulsī, pulsum to pluck
Line 16:	**nīl** = *nihil*; direct object of *sonat*.
	humilis, humile slight
	ēnervis, ēnerve weakened, enfeebled
	sublīmis, sublīme lifted up, raised up; modifies *lyra* in line 15.
Line 17:	**vexō** (1) to move violently, shake, agitate, harass; epexegetic infinitive dependent on *sublīmis et audāx*.
Line 18:	**agitō** (1) to disturb, assail with reproach
	vitium, -(i)ī, n. fault, flaw
Lines 18–21:	**sīve ... sīve** whether ... or; correlatives
Lines 18–19:	**agitās vitium ... mordēs commissa:** Note the parallel structure and the SYNCHESIS, both of which connect closely the misdeeds to the misbehaving youth.

LIEVEN DE MEYERE *LIBER* 1, *ODE* 6, CONTINUED

Cēnsor, et errantis mordēs commissa iuventae,

20   Mōrum perītus arbiter:

Aurea sīve canis

Observanda sacrīs quondam praecepta poētīs,

Nōn posterīs exactius

Graecia līquit opus:

25   Aut Maecēnātī sī cōmis epistola fertur

Legenda vel Nerōnibus;

Omnia plēna Deō,

Grātiaque ūtilitāsque comesque ambōbus honestum;

Decorque quī vulgum latet,

30   Sīdereusque furor

NOTES AND VOCABULARY

Line 19:   **cēnsor, cēnsoris,** m. critic, judge; appositive to the subject of *agitās* in line 18 and *mordēs* in line 19.

mordeō, mordēre, momordī, morsum to bite, sting, vex, attack

commissum, -ī, n. transgression, fault

iuventa, -ae, f. youth

Line 20:   **mos, mōris,** n. custom; *mōrum* is an objective genitive with *perītus*.

perītus, -a, -um skilled, experienced ("experienced in human behavior")

arbiter, -trī, m. judge, arbiter

Line 21:   **aurea:** The word reminds readers of Horace's *auream ... mediocritātem* in *Odes* 2.10. It is placed at the beginning of the line for emphasis and modifies *praecepta* in the next stanza. Note the HYPERBATON.

canō, canere, cecinī, cantum to sing, sing about; be careful to distinguish between the second singular present active of the verb *canō* and the noun *canis, canis,* m./f. "dog."

Line 22:   **observanda:** verbal adjective; translate "to be ...."

sacrīs ... poētīs: dative of agent; note the SYNCHESIS.

praeceptum, -ī, n. rule, precept

Line 23:	**posterī, -ōrum,** m. pl. coming generations, posterity
	exactius: comparative neuter adjective of *exactus, -a, -um*, precise, exact; modifies *opus* in line 24. Note the emphasis placed on *exactius* and *opus* by their position at the end of successive lines (cf. Sarbiewski, lines 9–10).
Line 24:	**linquō, linquere, līquī** to leave
Line 25:	**Maecēnas, Maecēnātis,** m. Maecenas was the patron of Horace as well as of Vergil.
	cōmis, cōme courteous, friendly; don't confuse this adjective with the noun *comes, comitis*, m./f. "companion" (see line 28) or *coma, -ae*, f. "hair."
Lines 25–26:	**aut . . . vel:** combination of the two correlatives. The pair *aut . . . aut* is used to indicate the choice must be one or the other; it cannot be both. *Vel . . . vel* gives both choices as possible. Thus, the poet seems to imply "to the Neros or to any other tyrant/poets of that type."
Line 26:	**legenda:** supply *est*; this is a passive periphrastic.
	Nerōnibus: "to Neros," i.e., to rulers, people in power
Line 27:	**plēnus, -a, -um** full of, filled with
	Deō: ablative of means with adjectives of filling, abounding, etc.
Line 28:	**grātia, -ae,** f. charm, grace
	comes, comitis, m. companion; appositive to *honestum*
	ambō, -ae, -ō both; dative with *comes*
	honestum, -ī, n. virtue, honesty, sincerity
Line 29:	**decor, decōris,** m. beauty
	vulgum, *adv.* (to) the general public; the poet has dropped the *in* from *in vulgum*.
	lateō, latēre, latuī to escape the notice of, be unknown to
Line 30:	**sīdereus, -a, -um** starry, heavenly
	furor, furōris, m. madness, frenzy

Singula dīvīnī sunt ornāmenta poētae,

Cui Rōma vix tulit parem,

Saecula nūlla ferent.

NOTES AND VOCABULARY

Line 31:   **singulī, -ae, -a** each one, all these

ornāmentum, -ī, n. ornament, badge, distinction, mark

Line 32:   **pār, paris** equal

Lines 32–33:   **Rōma . . . tulit parem** and **saecula . . . ferent:** Note the parallel structure in the last two lines. This enables the reader to supply the missing words in line 33, i.e., "To whom no age will bear an equal." Note, also, how the verb changes to the future and makes the praise even greater.

Line 33:   **saeculum, -ī,** n. age

COMPREHENSION QUESTIONS

1. What does the author of this poem consider Horace powerful enough to do? Cite the Latin.

2. What does the author credit Horace with adapting?

3. According to the author, what is Horace's lyre bold enough to do? Cite the Latin.

4. What qualities are marks of a divine poet?

Orpheus amongst the Thracians. The legendary singer and musician, Orpheus, is here portrayed among two men from his homeland of Thrace; Attic red-figure bell-krater. (©Wikimedia Commons)

READING 18

Mathias Casimir Sarbiewski (1595–1649) is celebrated as the "Horace of Poland." The citizens of his hometown memorialize their favorite son with a regular festival of poetry. As a young man he became a Jesuit and studied at the college in Vilnius, Lithuania (at that time, Poland and Lithuania were united). He completed his studies in Rome, was ordained a priest, and returned to his alma mater where he taught rhetoric, philosophy, and theology for a decade. He was then appointed personal preacher to King Wladislaw IV with whom he spent four years as travel companion as well as preacher. Sarbiewski was talented in and enjoyed the fine arts, especially music. His treatises include such subjects as theology, the ancient arts and sciences, and angels. He demonstrated a remarkable gift as a poet and is said to have mastered all the meters of the ancients. Sarbiewski composed poems about a variety of subjects from the theological to the patriotic. The latter probably inspired King Wladislaw to proclaim him poet laureate of Poland. A volume of his poems translated into English was published in 1646.

The "Horace of Poland" is reputed to have known all of Horace's odes by heart. Sarbiewski also admired the lyrical works of the Greek poet Pindar, who greatly influenced his own compositions. Sarbiewski was known to balance his time in the courts of his influential and wealthy patrons with periods of solitude and reflection. This ode to his ancestral home speaks to that balance as he savors the simple joys of the natural world and celebrates his beloved Fons Sona. His poem consciously echoes Horace's *Odes* 3.13, which celebrates Horace's beloved *Fons Bandusiae*. Note the allusion in lines 1–2 and 19. Sarbiewski alludes to Catullus's poem to Sirmio, that poet's island refuge, in lines 4–6 and 20.

Pope Urban VIII who celebrated the glorification of his reign with a magnificent fresco in the grand hall of his palace in Rome. Bernini depicts his patron seated on the papal throne, crowned with the triple papal tiara, and addressing the people as connoted by Urban's outstretched hand. Artists of the baroque like Bernini helped the Popes wage the Counter Reformation as they dazzled with the grandeur of their churches and decoration. (© Wikimedia Commons)

THERE'S NO PLACE LIKE HOME ....

MATHIAS CASIMIR SARBIEWSKI *LIBER EPODON*, 2 AD FONTEM SONAM

Meter: Iambic strophe

In patriō fundō

1   Fōns innocentī lūcidus magis vītrō,

     Pūrāque pūrior nive,

    Pāgī voluptās, ūna Nymphārum sitis,

     Ocelle nātālis solī,

5   Longīs viārum languidus labōribus,

     Et mōle cūrārum gravis

    Tuscīs ab usque gentibus redux, tibi

     Acclīne prōsternō latus.

NOTES AND VOCABULARY

Title: **fōns, fontis,** m. spring, fountain, source

       Sona, -ae, f. most probably the spring in Sarbiewski's ancestral home or village

       patrius, -a, -um father's, ancestral

       fundus, -ī, m. estate

Line 1:   **innocēns, innocentis** faultless, spotless

       lūcidus, -a, -um clear, bright, shining

       magis more

       vītrum, -ī, n. glass

Line 2:   Note the POLYPTOTON.

       nix, nivis, f. snow

Line 3:   **pāgus, -ī,** m. village, a country district

       voluptās, voluptātis, f. enjoyment, pleasure

       Nymphārum: subjective genitive; translate *ūna . . . sitis* "the one thirst of the Nymphs (the only thing for which the Nymphs thirst [long for])"

       sitis, sitis, f. thirst

Line 4:   **ocelle:** *lit.,* "little eye": jewel; translate "the light of my eye."

          nātālis, nātāle native

          solum, -ī, n. ground, soil, land

Line 5:   **viārum:** *lit.,* "of the roads"; translate "journey."

          languidus, -a, -um exhausted

Lines 5–6: The SYNCHESIS illustrates the tight connection between the long journey and the burden of cares, both of which made him so weary. Note the effect of the ALLITERATION.

Line 6:   **mōlēs, mōlis,** f. mass, burden

Line 7:   **Tuscus, -a, -um** Etruscan; the position of *Tuscīs* at the beginning of the line instead of *redux* emphasizes where the traveler has been (and how far away) rather than the fact of his return.

          usque, *adv.* all the way

          gēns, gentis, f. people, nation

          Tuscīs gentibus: refers to the environs of Rome

          redux, reducis coming back, returning

          tibi: dative of possession (emphasizing the possession, rather than the possessor; *tibi latus* = you have the bank)

Line 8:   **acclīne prōsternō latus:** *lit.,* "I throw (myself) in front of your inclined side"; translate "I fall prostrate on your sloping side."

          latus, lateris, n. side, bank

          acclīne latus: accusative, direct object of *prōsternō.* The "inclined side" is the bank of the spring.

MATHIAS CASIMIR SARBIEWSKI *LIBER EPODON*, 2 AD FONTEM SONAM, CONTINUED

Permitte siccus, quā potes, premī; cavā

10   Permitte lībārī manū,

Sīc tē quiētum nūlla perturbet pecus,

      Rāmusve lāpsus arbore:

Sīc, dum loquācī prāta garritū secās,

      Et laetus audīrī salīs,

15   Assibilantēs pōpulētōrum comae

      Ingrāta pōnant murmura

Tibī lyraeque vātis. Haud frūstrā sacer

      Nam sī quid Urbānus probat,

NOTES AND VOCABULARY

Line 9:   **siccus, -a, -um** dry, thirsty

        quā potes (supply *viā*): *lit.*, "by which way you are able"; translate "however you are able."

        premī: "to be pressed, to be overcome." Note that both *premī* and *lībārī* are passive in form. They act here like Greek middles, which means they affect their subjects. Sarbiewski was an admirer of Pindar and he no doubt knew his Greek well. This construction would also explain the nominative of *siccus,* which must modify the poet and not the spring, which is feminine and the subject of *permitte*. Translate "Permit me to suppress my thirst, permit me to drink with my hollow hand."

        cavā: modifies *manū* in line 10. Note that these two words are both placed at the end of their lines for emphasis.

Line 10:   **lībō** (1) to drink

Lines 9–10: Note the ANAPHORA.

Line 11:   **tē quiētum:** *lit.*, "you quiet"; translate "your rest (peace)"

        perturbō (1) to disturb; present optative subjunctive; translate "May no sheep disturb."

        pecus, pecudis, f. sheep; be sure to distinguish between this word and *pecus, pecoris,* n. "flock" and *pectus, pectoris,* n. "heart."

Line 12:   **rāmus, -ī,** m. branch

        lābor, lābī, lāpsus sum to slide, slip, fall

Lines 11–13:	Note the ANAPHORA.

Line 13: **loquāx, loquācis** talkative; note how the two words describing the babbling sound of the spring waters "surround" the word for "meadows" as their murmur "surrounds" (can be heard all over) the fields.

prātum, -ī, n. meadow

garritus, -ūs, m. chattering

secō (1) to cut, pass through

Line 14: **laetus, -a, -um** happy; modifies the subject of *secās* and *salīs.*

saliō, salīre, saluī, saltum to leap

Line 15: **assibilō** (1) to hiss, murmur; translate "rustling"; note the ONOMATOPOEIA and SIBILANCE.

pōpulētum, -ī, n. plantation or stand of poplar trees

coma, -ae, f. hair, foliage

Line 16: **ingrātus, -a, -um** unpleasing

pōnō, pōnere, posuī, positum to lay aside; optative subjunctive ("may they lay aside"); note the ALLITERATION and the ONOMATOPOEIA.

Line 17: **lyrae:** dative singular

vātēs, vātis, m./f. bard, poet

haud, *adv.* hardly, scarcely

frūstrā, *adv.* in vain; note the LITOTES.

Line 18: **quid** = *aliquid*; remember that "after *sī, nisi, num,* and *nē,* all the *ali's* fall away."

Urbānus: Pope Urban VIII (1568–1644; pope 1621–1644) was himself a poet and a patron of Sarbiewski. In several of his odes, Sarbiewski celebrated Pope Urban VIII as his Maecenas. Urban's nephew, Cardinal Francis Barberini, was another of his patrons in Rome. Urban VIII was a great patron of the arts commissioning the baroque master Bernini, to sculpt the Fountain of the Triton, the baldacchino over the main altar in St. Peter's Basilica, and the pope's mausoleum that stands in St. Peter's.

Lines 18–20: **sī . . . probat . . . dēbeās:** This is a mixed condition. The poet knows definitely that Pope Urban does not approve of anything in vain, but, even so, the poet is not sure of gaining equal status with Catullus and Horace. Translate *dēbeās* "you may owe . . . ."

MATHIAS CASIMIR SARBIEWSKI *LIBER EPODON*, 2 AD FONTEM SONAM, CONTINUED

Ōlim fluentī lēne Blauduiae nihil,

20   Aut Sirmiōnī dēbeās.

NOTES AND VOCABULARY

Line 19:   **ōlim,** *adv.* some day

              fluō, fluere, flūxī, fluxum flow

              lēne: the neuter accusative is here used adverbially; translate "gently."

              Blauduiae = *Bandusiae,* the spring made famous by Horace in *Odes* 3.13.

Line 20:   **Sirmiōnī** = *Sirmio,* the island on Lake Garda in northern Italy made famous by Catullus in Poem 31

COMPREHENSION QUESTIONS

1. From where had the author just returned?

2. What does the author want to do after his return?

3. To what does the author compare Sona in lines 19–20?

APPENDIX A

LATIN METERS

The meters of Latin poetry derive from those of Greek poetry and are constructed on patterns of long and short syllables. Determining whether syllables are long or short and marking their quantity is called "scansion."

In Latin, every syllable contains a vowel or a diphthong; a diphthong combines two vowels that make a single sound, such as the "au" in *laudō* or the "ae" in *puellae*. A Latin word contains as many syllables as it has vowels or diphthongs. So, *me-a* has two syllables; *ā-ri-dō* has three. A syllable whose quantity is long (i.e., a long mark [macron] appears over the vowel) takes longer to read than a syllable whose quantity is short (i.e., the vowel lacks a macron). For this reason meters in classical poetry are referred to as "quantitative verse." It should be noted that when "u" is combined with "q" or "g," the "u" in "qu" and "gu" is not counted as a separate syllable. So, *e-quus* and *a-qua* have two syllables; *san-gui-ne-us* has four.

DETERMINATION OF A VOWEL'S LENGTH

- All diphthongs (ae, au, ei, eu, oe, and ui) are long **by nature**.

- All vowels marked by a macron are long **by nature**. For example, the "a" in the first syllable of *māter* is long by nature because a long mark (macron) appears over the vowel, while the "e" in the second syllable is short by nature because the vowel lacks a macron.

- Short vowels may become long **by position**. If a syllable containing a short vowel is followed by two or more consonants or a double consonant "x" (pronounced cs) or "z" (pronounced ds), the syllable is considered long by position. In a line of poetry, the short "i" of *ignem* becomes long by position because the vowel is followed by two consonants. This rule also applies to a short vowel followed by a single consonant in the final syllable of a word, where the short vowel is considered long if the next word begins with a consonant. For example, in the phrase *miser Catulle*, the "e" in *miser* becomes long by position because "r" is followed by a consonant ("C"), and the entire phrase should be marked ‿ – ‿ – ‿. The vowel in the syllable lengthened by position is still pronounced short.

TWO DOUBLE CONSONANT EXCEPTIONS

- If a short syllable is followed by a consonant cluster that involves a mute (b, c, d, g, p, t) and a liquid (l or r), the syllable may be long or short. The quantity of the syllable will depend on what the metrical scheme requires.

- For the purposes of scansion, the letter "h" should not be regarded as a consonant, and so will not lengthen the quality of a vowel if the word or syllable that precedes it ends in a single consonant. For example, in the phrase *quidquid hoc libellī*, the second syllable of *quidquid* is short because the "h" of *hoc* is disregarded. Similarly, in the word *anhēlitus*, the first syllable, "an" is marked or scanned as short because the *"an-"* is followed by an "h."

TWO RULES ABOUT WORDS ENDING IN A VOWEL OR –M

- **Elision**, derived from the Latin verb *elidō*, which means "to knock out" or "to eliminate," takes place when a vowel, diphthong, or a vowel plus "–m" ends one word and is followed by a word beginning with an "h," a vowel, or a diphthong. In the following examples, note how the final vowel or vowel + "m" is "knocked out" and how the word is combined with the next word in which the initial "h" also may be eliminated. The opening words of line 8 of Catullus Poem 1, *quare habe*, illustrate the elimination of both a vowel ("e") and an "h": through elision *quare habe* becomes: *quārē habē*. In line 554 of Vergil's *Aeneid* 2, the "–um" of *fātōrum* and *hic* come together to create: *fātōrum hic* (*fātōric*). In line 268 of Book 10 of Ovid's *Metamorphōsēs*, the "–am" of *sociam* and the "ac–" of *acclīnātaque* produce the following elision: *sociam adclīnātatque* (*sociadclīnātaque*). The most common type of elision, however, involves eliminating the final vowel of one word before combining that word with the next word that begins with a vowel as in this example from *Aeneid* 1, line 424: *mōlīrī arcem*.

- **Prodelision** is a special form of elision that applies to only two Latin words, *es* and *est*. When these verbs follow a word ending in a vowel, diphthong, or a vowel combined with "–m," the "e" of *es* or *est* is eliminated instead of the final vowel, diphthong, or the vowel combined with "–m" of the preceding word. For example, in line 281 of Ovid, *Metamorphōsēs* Book 10, the "e" in *est* is eliminated in eliding *tepēre* and *est*: *tepēre (e)st*. In line 13 of Catullus 51, the "e" in *est* is eliminated in eliding *molestum* and *est*: *molestumst*. Prodelision, then, is the opposite of elision in that it eliminates the vowel in *es* and *est* and retains the final vowel, diphthong, or the vowel combined with "–m" of the preceding word.

METERS

In Latin poetry, a foot is a metrical unit of at least two syllables. Look at the following examples of feet, each of which has its own name.

		$-\cup\cup$
dactyl	$-\cup\cup$	cētera
		$--$
spondee	$--$	rēgēs
		$\cup\cup-$
anapest	$\cup\cup-$	superant
		$-\cup$
trochee	$-\cup$	mēnsa
		$\cup-$
iamb	$\cup-$	amō
		$-\cup\cup-$
choriamb	$-\cup\cup-$	sanguineae

Dactylic Hexameter: The meter of ancient epic, the dactylic hexameter begins with Homer. Vergil used this meter in composing the *Aeneid*, and Ovid used the same meter for his epic, the *Metamorphōsēs*. The dactylic hexameter consists of six feet. A line of dactylic hexameter could be considered as consisting of a pattern of five consecutive feet made up of dactyls ($-\cup\cup$), with the sixth foot consisting of a long syllable and an anceps (×). The *syllaba anceps* indicates that the final syllable can be either long or short. The first four feet allow a substitution of a spondee (– –); the fifth foot is nearly always a dactyl. The metrical pattern for a dactylic hexameter line, then, looks like this:

$$– \overline{\smile\smile} \mid – \overline{\smile\smile} \mid – \overline{\smile\smile} \mid – \overline{\smile\smile} \mid – \smile\smile \mid – ×$$
$$1 \qquad 2 \qquad 3 \qquad 4 \qquad 5 \qquad 6$$

Several examples of the hexameter line follow; two lines are taken from Vergil and two from Ovid.

$$– \quad \smile\smile – \smile\smile – \quad – \quad – \quad – \smile\smile \quad – \quad ×$$

sanguine|ae supe|rant un|dās; pars| cētera| pontum

(Vergil *Aeneid* 2.208)

$$– \smile\smile – \smile\smile – \quad – \quad – \smile\smile – \smile\smile \quad – \quad ×$$

pōne le|git sinu|atque im|mēnsa vo| lūmine| terga

(Vergil *Aeneid* 2.209)

$$– \quad – \quad – \smile\smile \quad – \quad \smile\smile – \smile\smile – \quad \smile\smile – ×$$

aut, hōc| sī nimi|um (e)st, vel ad| ōscula danda pa|tērēs?

(Ovid *Metamorphōsēs* 4.75)

$$– \smile \smile – \quad – \quad – \smile\smile \quad – \quad – \quad – \smile \smile – \quad ×$$

nec sumus| ingrā|tī: tibi| nōs dē|bēre fa|tēmur,

(Ovid *Metamorphōsēs* 4.76)

The Elegiac Couplet: Poems 65–116 of Catullus are written in elegiac couplets. This meter consists of two lines of poetry, a line of a dactylic hexameter (six feet) followed by a line of dactylic pentameter (five feet). The pentameter line is made up of two units of two and a half feet each; a pause in the middle of the third foot after the long syllable marks a break in the line. Spondees may substitute for dactyls in the first two feet. The second half of the line is fixed, however, with the 4th and 5th feet consisting only of dactyls, followed by a long syllable. Here is the pattern for the pentameter line:

− ⏖ | − ⏖ | − ‖ − ⏑ ⏑ | − ⏑ ⏑ | −

  1   2   ½   4   5   ½

Two examples of elegiac couplets follow, taken from Poem 107 of Catullus.

  −   −   −   −   −   −   −   −   −⏑⏑ − ×

quārē hoc| est grā| tum nō |bīsque est| cārius| aurō

   −   −   − ⏑ ⏑ −   − ⏑⏑   − ⏑ ⏑ −

Quod tē| restitu| is, ‖ Lesbia,| mī cupid|ō.

(Catullus, *Carmen* 107.3–4)

− ⏑ ⏑ − ⏑ ⏑   −   −   −−   − ⏑ ⏑ − ×

restitu|is cupi|dō atque īn|spēran|tī, ipsa re|fers tē

    − − − − −   − ⏑ ⏑ −⏑ ⏑ −

nōbīs| ō lūc|em ‖ candidi|ōre no| tā!

(Catullus, *Carmen* 107.5–6)

Sapphic Stanza: Sappho of Lesbos, a celebrated Greek poetess of the sixth century BCE, gives her name to the Sapphic meter, which she apparently invented. Catullus composed only two poems in this meter, which happen to be two of his most famous Lesbia poems, Poems 11 and 51. Horace, on the other hand, composed many of his lyric poems in the Sapphic meter, including *Odes* 1.22 and 2.10. This meter forms a stanza or strophe of four lines each. The first three lines repeat the same pattern, in which the choliamb (− ⏑ ⏑ −) forms the centerpiece. Catullus allows either a short or a long in the fourth syllable of the line (marked below as an anceps), while in Horace's Sapphic stanzas that syllable is always long. The pattern for the first three lines is this:

− ⏑ − × | − ⏑ ⏑ − | ⏑ − ×

The fourth line of the stanza consists of five syllables that make up two feet, the first of which is a dactyl and the second of which may be either a spondee or a trochee. Since the last syllable may be long or short, this syllable is marked as an anceps: − ⏑ ⏑ | − ×. The first example that follows is taken from Catullus, Poem 51, the second from Horace, *Odes* 1.22.

$-\breve{}- \quad \breve{} \quad -\breve{}\,\breve{}- \quad \breve{}- \quad \times$

ōtium Ca| tulle tibi| molestum (e)st

$-\breve{}- \quad -\quad -\quad \breve{}\,\breve{}- \quad \breve{}- \times$

ōtiō exsul|tās nimium|que gestis

$-\breve{} \quad -\quad -\quad -\quad \breve{}\,\breve{}- \quad \breve{}-\times$

ōti(um) et rē|gēs prius et| beātās

$-\breve{}\,\breve{} \quad -\times$

perdidit| urbēs

    (Catullus 51.13–16)

$-\quad \breve{}-\quad -\quad -\quad \breve{}\,\breve{}-\quad \breve{}\quad -\times$

Integer vī| tae sceleris| que pūrus

$-\quad \breve{}-\quad -\quad -\breve{}\,\breve{}-\quad \breve{}\quad -\quad \times$

nōn eget Mau| rīs iaculīs| neque arcū

$-\quad \breve{}--\quad -\quad \breve{}\,\breve{}-\quad \breve{}-\times$

nec venēnā| tīs gravidā| sagittīs

$-\quad \breve{}\quad \breve{}-\times$

Fūsce, phra| retrā,

    (Horace *Odes* 1.22.1–4)

The Second Asclepiadean: Horace, *Odes* 1.3, the poem for Vergil, is written in the second Asclepiadean. Pairs of lines follow this metrical scheme:

$--\,|-\breve{}\,\breve{}-\,|\,\breve{}\times$

$--\,|-\breve{}\,\breve{}-\,|-\breve{}\,\breve{}-\,|\,\breve{}\times$

Note that the center of each line is made up of choriamb or a pair of choriambs $(-\breve{}\,\breve{}-)$. An example of this meter follows.

$$- \quad - \quad -\cup \quad \cup - \qquad \cup \ \times$$

Sīc tē| dīva potēns | Cyprī

$$- \quad - \quad - \quad \cup\cup - \quad -\cup\cup - \ \cup\times$$

Sīc frā| trēs Helenae || lūcida sī|dera

(Horace *Odes* 1.3.1–2)

Lieven De Meyer's poem is written in an unusual meter, three-line stanzas, consisting of a first line of a dactylic hexameter; a second line of an iambic dimeter ($\cup - \cup - \cup - \cup \times$)—note the first foot may also be a spondee ($- \ -$) or an anapest ($\cup \ \cup -$); and a third line of a dactylic catalectic trimester ($- \cup \cup - \cup \cup -$).

$$- \quad \cup \ \cup - \ - \quad - \quad \cup \quad \cup - \qquad - \ - \ \cup\cup \ - \times$$

Flacce, lyrā cantūque potēns haerentia vīvis

$$- \ - \cup - \ \cup \ - \cup \ \times$$

Movēre saxa rūpibus,

$$-\cup\cup- \qquad \cup \ \cup \ \times$$

Thrĕiciumque nemus

(*Odes* 6, *Liber* 1, 1–3)

Sarbiewski's poem, *Epode* 2, is written in iambic strophes that follow this pattern:

Line 1: $\times - \cup - \times - \cup - \times - \times \times$

Line 2: $\times - \cup - \times - \cup \times$

$$- \quad - \quad \cup - \ --\cup \ - \qquad \cup - \ \times \ \times$$

Fōns innocentī lūcidus magis vītrō,

$$- \ - \quad \cup \ -\cup- \ \cup \ \times$$

Pūrāque pūrior nive,

(*Epode* 2, 1–2)

APPENDIX B

RHETORICAL TERMS

ALLITERATION

Repetition of the same letter (usually initial) in a series of two or more words.

> Example: *receptōs ad sē sociōs sibi ascīscunt.*
> (Caesar *Dē bellō Gallicō*, 1.5.17)

ANAPHORA

A word(s) is repeated for emphasis at the beginning of a series of phrases or clauses.

> Example: *dein mīlle altera, dein secunda centum, / deinde usque*
> *altera mīlle, deinde centum / dein, cum mīlia multa*
> *fēcerīmus.*
> (Catullus Poem 5.8–10)

ASSONANCE

The same or similar vowel sounds are repeated in neighboring words.

> Example: *līliaquē pictāsque lapsās et ab arbore lāpsās*
> (Ovid *Metamorphōsēs* 10. 262)

ASYNDETON

The omission of a connective such as *et* or *–que.*

> Example: *Hī omnēs linguā, institūtīs, (et) lēgibus inter sē differunt.*
> (Caesar *Dē bellō Gallicō* 1.1.2–3)

CHIASMUS

An A-B-B-A arrangement of pairs of words.

> Example: *Vīvāmus, mea Lesbia, atque amēmus.*
> (Catullus Poem 5.1)

ELLIPSIS

One or more words are needed to complete the thought in one or more clauses.

> Example: *Gallia est omnis dīvīsa in partēs trēs, quārum ūnam incolunt Belgae.*
> (Caesar *Dē bellō Gallicō* 1.1.1)

EPITHET

A descriptive word or phrase about a character, hero, or location with which the author emphasizes a characteristic of the person or place.

> Example: *īnsignem pietāte virum.*
> (Vergil *Aeneid* 1.10)

EUPHEMISM

An expression in which something less offensive or disagreeable is substituted for something more offensive or disagreeable; often used in reference to death.

> Example: *sub terrās ībit.*
> (Vergil *Aeneid* 4.654).

FIGŪRA ETYMOLOGICA (PARANOMASIA)

A play on two words based on their common derivation.

> Example: *Clōdiā, muliere nōn sōlum nōbilī vērum etiam nōtā.*
> (Cicero *Prō Caeliō* 13.16)

GOLDEN LINE

A line of dactylic hexameter consisting of a pair of adjacent adjectives and a pair of adjacent nouns, with a verb separating the two pairs in an A- B- Verb A- B- or A- B- Verb B- A- arrangement of words.

Example: *et scelerāta ferō cōnsūmite vīscera morsū.*
                   (Ovid *Metamorphōsēs* 4.113)

HENDIADYS

Two nouns linked by a conjunction express one idea.

Example: *bellī atque fortitūdinis.*
                   (Caesar *Dē bellō Gallicō* 1.2.10–11)

HYPERBATON

The separation of words that belong together.

Example: *paucīs, sī tibi dī favent, diēbus.*
                   (Catullus Poem 13.2)

HYPERBOLE

Exaggeration for effect.

Example: *hūius urbis atque adeō dē orbis terrārum exitiō cōgitent.*
                   (Cicero *In Catilīnam* 1.4.10).

IRONY

One thing is said but the opposite is meant.

Example: *Nōs autem, fortēs virī, satis facere reī pūblicae vidēmur,*
                   sī istīus furōrem ac tēla vītāmus.
                   (Cicero *In Catilīnam* 1.2.11–12)

LITOTES

Understatement; frequently found with a double negative.

Example: *neque abest suspiciō.*
                   (Caesar *Dē Bellō Gallicō* 1.4.7)

METAPHOR

A comparison made without using the words "like" or "as."

Example: *quot ego tuās petitiōnēs ita coniectās ut vītārī posse nōn vidērentur parvā quādam dēclīnātiōne et, ut aiunt, corpore effūgī!*
(Cicero *In Catilīnam* 1.6.3–4)

METONYMY

One word is used for another with which it is closely associated.

Example: *quōs ferrō trucīdārī oportēbat.*
(Cicero *In Catilīnam* 1.4.11)

ONOMATOPOEIA

The sound of the word(s) suggests the actual sound.

Example: *tintinant aurēs.*
(Catullus Poem 51.11)

PERSONIFICATION (PROSOPOPOEIA)

Human qualities are attributed to objects or an absent or imagery person is represented as speaking.

Example: *aliquis mihi ab īnferīs excitandus est ex barbātīs illīs, . . . quī obiūrget mulierem et quī prō mē loquātur . . . .*
(Cicero *Prō Caeliō*, 14.33–34.17–19)

POLYPTOTON

Words from the same base/root, but in a different form, appear in close proximity.

Example: *ars adeō latet arte suā.*
(Ovid *Metamorphōsēs* 10.252)

POLYSYNDETON

Many connectives in close succession, where one or more could be omitted.

Example: *et Rauracīs et Tulingīs et Latōbrigīs.*
(Caesar *Dē bellō Gallicō* 1.5.14–15)

RHETORICAL QUESTION

A question is asked but an answer is not expected.

Example: *quae tibi manet vīta? / quis nunc te adībit? cui vidēberis bella? / quem nunc amābis? cūius esse dīcēris? / quem bāsiābis? cui labella mordēbis?*
        (Catullus Poem 8.15–18)

SIBILANCE

The repetition of the "s" sound; this is a form of alliteration.

Example: *rūmōrēsque senum sevēriōrum / omnēs ūnius aestimēmus assis!*
        (Catullus Poem 5.2–3)

SIMILE

An analogy or comparison is made using a word for "like" or "as."

Example: *Ut saepe hominēs aegrī morbō gravī, cum aestū febrīque iactantur, sī aquam gelidam bibērunt, prīmō relevātī videntur, deinde multō gravius vehementiusque afflictantur, sīc hīc morbus quī est in rē pūblicā relevātus istīus poenā vehementius reliquīs vīvīs ingravēscet.*
        (Cicero *In Catilīnam* 1.13.5–8)

SYNCHESIS (INTERLOCKED WORD ORDER)

An A-B-A-B arrangement of words.

Example: *saevae memorem Iūnōnis ob īram.*
        (Vergil *Aeneid* 1.4)

SYNECDOCHE

Part of something is used to represent the whole or the whole is used to represent a part.

Example: *ā tēctīs urbis ac moenibus.*
        (Cicero *In Catilīnam* 1.13.24)

TMESIS

The separation of the parts of a compound word into two distinct words.

Example: *bis medium amplexī, bis collō squāmea circum /*
            terga datī superant capite et cervīcibus altīs.
            (Vergil *Aeneid* 2.218–219)

TRANSFERRED EPITHET

A word describing an essential quality of one word that grammatically modifies a different word.

Example: *gemina teguntur / lūmina nocte.*
            (Catullus Poem 51.11–12)

TRICOLON

Three words, phrases, or clauses arranged in a particular order; anaphora often is used to mark off a set of three.

Example: *nōn feram, nōn patiar, nōn sinam.*
            (Cicero *In Catilīnam* 1.5.28)

LATIN TO ENGLISH GLOSSARY

A

ā, ab, *prep. + abl.* from, by

abavus, -ī, m. great-great-grandfather

abscindō, -ere, abscidī, abscissum to tear away, cut off

absum, abesse, afuī, afutūrum to refrain, be absent from

ac, *conj.* and

accidō, -ere, accidī to occur, happen to (+ *dat. of person affected*)

accipiō, -ere, -cēpī, -ceptum to receive

accommodō (1) (+ *dat.*) to adjust, apply

accūsātor, -ōris, m. accuser, prosecutor

Acherōn, Acherontis/Acherontos, m. A mythical river or lake that separates the world of the living from the world of the dead, often identified with the river Styx

Ācroceraunia, -ōrum, n. a very dangerous rocky promontory on the coast of Epirus that runs out into the Ionian Sea

addō, -dere, -didī, -ditum to add

addūcō, -ere, addūxī, adductum to lead toward, bring in; influence

adferō, adferre, attulī, adlātum to bring or carry to a place

adficiō, -ere, adfēcī, adfectum to affect, impair

adfīnis, -e related by marriage

adfor (1) to address, accost

adhibeō, -ēre, adhibuī, adhibitum (+ *dat.*) to invite, summon

aditus, -ūs, m. approach, encounter

adloquor, adloquī, adlocūtus sum to address, accost

administer, administrī, m. assistant

admiror (1) to admire, respect, be surprised (at), be astonished (at)

admodum, *adv.* very, quite, just about

adsistō, -ere, adstitī *or* **asistī** to stand near

a(d)spectus, -ūs, m. sight, vision, aspect

a(d)spiciō, a(d)spicere, a(d)spexī to see, look at

adulēscēns, adulēscentis, m./f. young man, young woman, youth

adulēscentulus, -ī, m. young man, youth

adulter, adulterī, m. illicit lover, paramour

adūrō, adūere, adussī, adustum to burn, scorch

adventus, -ūs, m. approach, arrival

aemulus, -a, -um vying with, rivaling

aequō (1) to equal(ize), match, reciprocate, level

aequor, aequoris, n. plain, delta, sea

āēr, āeris, m. air

aes, aeris, n. bronze

aes aliēnum, aeris aliēnī, n. debt

aesculētum, -ī, n. oak forest

aestīvus, -a, -um summer

aestuōsus, -a, -um sweltering, very hot, agitated

aetas, aetātis, f. age

aethēr, aetheris, m. sky, air

aetherius, -a, -um heavenly

Āfricus, -ī, m. the southwest wind

agitō (1) to disturb, assail with reproach

agnōscō, -ere, agnōvī, agnitum to recognize

agō, -ere, ēgī, āctum to do, drive, treat

āles, ālitis, m./f. bird

aliēnus, -a, -um that which belongs to another

aliquī, aliqua, aliquod, *indefinite adj.,* some

aliquis, aliquid some, someone, anyone, something, anything

alligō (1) to tie, fasten

āla, -ae, f. wing

alō, -ere, aluī, altum to nourish

Alpēs, Alpium, f. pl. Alps

alter . . . alter the one . . . the other

alter, altera, alterum one (of two)

amantissimus, -a, -um most loving, most beloved, most dear

ambactus, -ī, m. vassal

ambāges, ambāgis, f. winding, evasion

ambō, -ae, -ō both

amīcitia, -ae, f. friendship

amīcus, -ī, m. friend

amor, amōris, m. love, love affair

amplus, -a, -um large, eminent, distinguished, powerful

an, *conj.* or

an(ne), *interrog.* whether, or

anima, -ae, f. soul

animus, -ī, m. mind, soul, heart

ante, *adv.* in front, before

antīquus, -a, -um ancient, old; ancestral

apud, *prep. + acc.* with, in the presence of, among

aqua, -ae, f. water; water supply, aqueduct

Aquilō, Aquilōnis, m. north wind, northeast wind, north-by-northeast wind

Arabs, Arabis, m. Arab

arātor, arātōris, m. a plowman

arātrum, -ī, n. plow

arbiter, -trī, m. judge, arbiter

arbitror (1) to consider, judge, think

Arctus, Arctī, f. bear; "the Bears" are Ursa Major and Ursa Minor (the Big and the Little Dipper)

arcus, arcūs, m. bow

ardeō, -ēre, arsī, — to burn

āridus, -a, -um dry

arx, arcis, f. citadel, hilltop, summit

a(d)spectus, -ūs, m. sight, vision, aspect

a(d)spiciō, a(d)spicere, a(d)spexī to see, look at

assibilō (1) to hiss, murmur

at, *conj.* but, yet

atavus, -ī, m. great-great-great grandfather

āter, ātra, ātrum black

atque, *conj.* and, and . . . yet

Atticus, -a, -um Attic, of the region of Attica, which surrounds the Greek city of Athens

auctor, auctōris, m./f. originator, supporter

auctōritās, auctōritātis, f. authority, power, influence

audāx, audācis (over)bold

audeō, -ēre, ausus sum to dare

aura, -ae, f. breeze

aurum, -ī, n. gold; thing(s) made of gold; gold ornaments

Ausōnius, -a, -um Italian; the Ausones were an indigenous people of central Italy

austērus, -a, -um (*of taste or smell*) harsh, severe, austere

autem, *adv.* however, moreover

avēna, -ae, f. stem, stalk

āvertō, -ere, āvertī, āversum to turn away, avert

avis, avis, f. bird

avītus, -a, -um of or pertaining to a grandfather; ancestral

avus, -ī, m. grandfather, ancestor

B

baculum, -ī, n. walking stick, staff

barbātus, -a, -um bearded

barbula, -ae, f. little beard, goatee

bidēns, bidentis sheep

biformis, -e two-formed, two-shaped

bis, *adv.* twice

C

cadō, -ere, cecidī, casum to fall, die

caecus, -a, -um blind

caedēs, caedis, f. death, slaughter, murder

caeles, caelitis, m./f. heaven-dweller, god

caelum, -ī, n. sky

caeruleus, -a, -um blue, greenish blue

calamitās, calamitātis, f. misfortune

Calymnē, -ēs, f. an island off the coast of Asia Minor near Rhodes

campus, -ī, m. plain, level surface; field

candēns, candentis shining, white, gleaming

canō, -ere, cecinī, cantum to sing, sing about

cantō (1) to sing, sing about, recite

cantus, -ūs, m. song

capiō, capere, cēpī, captum to take

captō (1) to try to catch

caput, capitis, n. head, chief, ringleader

carmen, carminis, n. song, poem

Carnūtes, Carnūtum, m. pl. a people in Gaul on both sides of the Loire

cārus, -a, -um dear

castra, -ōrum, n. (military) camp

cāsus, -ūs, m. chance, (mis)fortune

Caucasus, -ī, m., Caucasus Mountains

causa, -ae, f. cause, case (at law), reason, occasion

causā + *gen.* for the sake of, because of

cautēs, cautis, f. rock, cliff, crag

Cecropidēs, -ae, m. *lit.* descendant of Cecrops (the first king of Athens), Athenian

cēdō, -ere, cessī, cessum to yield, depart

celebrō (1) to frequent

celsus, -a, -um high, lofty

cēnsor, cēnsoris, m. critic, judge

cēra, -ae, f. wax

certus, -a, -um, certain, sure, specific

Chalcidicus, -a, -um Chalcidian, from Chalcis

cieō, ciēre, cīvī, citum to stir (up), (a) rouse

circā, *adv.* around, about

circā, *prep.* + *acc.* around

circumveniō, -īre, circumvēnī, circumventum to enclose, surround

circumvolō (1) to fly around, fly about

clam, *adv.* secretly, in secret, covertly

clārus, -a, -um bright, clear, famous

claudō, -ere, clausī, clausum to close, enclose

Cleopatra, -ae, f. Cleopatra

clīvus, -ī, m. slope, incline

coepī, coepisse, coeptum to have begun

coeptum, -ī, n. design, undertaking

cognātus, -a, -um related, kindred

cōgnōscō, -ere, cōgnōvī, cōgnitum to know, learn

cōgō, -ere, coēgī, coāctum to force (together), compel

cohors, cohortis, f. throng, cohort, crowd

colōrō (1) color, stain

coma, -ae, f. hair, foliage

comes, comitis, m./f. companion, comrade

cōmis, -e courteous, friendly

comitō (1) to go along, accompany, attend

comitor (1) to accompany, attend, escort, follow

commissum, -ī, n. transgression, fault

committō, -ere, commīsī, commissum to commit, entrust

commodō (1) to lend, loan

commoveō, -ēre, commōvī, commōtum to move, sway

commūnicō (1) to share

complector, complectī, complexus sum to embrace, hug; seize

compleō, -ēre, complēvī, complētum to fill, complete

complūrēs, complūrium several

comprehendō, -ere, comprehendī, comprehēnsum to capture, arrest, to seize

concurrō, -ere, concurrī, concursum (+ *ad*) to flock (to) in crowds, to assemble together

concutiō, -ere, concussī, concussum to shake, shatter, agitate

condō, -ere, condidī, conditum to found, establish, put away, store

cōnficiō, -ere, cōnfēcī, cōnfectum to complete

cōnfīdō, -ere, cōnfīsus sum (+ *dat.*) to rely on, trust

coniūnctus, -a, -um connected, friendly

coniūnx, coniūgis, m./f. spouse

conloquor, conloquī, conlocūtus sum to speak with

cōnor (1) to try, attempt

conpōnō, -ere, conposuī, conpositum to join, place together

cōnscendō, -ere, cōnscendī, cōnscēnsum to board, go on board

cōnsecrō (1) to consecrate, dedicate to the gods

cōnsīdō, -ere, cōnsēdī, cōnsessum to hold sessions, encamp, settle

consilium, -(i)ī, n. council, deliberation, decision, planning

cōnstituō, -ere, cōnstituī, cōnstitūtum to decide, determine, judge; establish

cōnsuēscō, -ere, cōnsuēvī, cōnsuētum to become accustomed to

cōnsul, cōnsulis, m. consul

contāgiō, contāgiōnis, f. contact

contendō, -ere, contendī, contentum to fight, compete

contexō, -ere, contexuī, contextum to weave together, entwine

contrōversia, -ae, f. dispute

contumēliōsus, -a, -um, abusive, insulting, outrageous, rude

convīcium, -(i)ī, n. a loud cry, shout; abuse, insult; reproach

copia, -ae, f. supply, abundance; (in the plural) forces, troops

corneus, -a, -um of horn

corripiō, -ere, corripuī, correptum to seize; hasten; to snatch (up, away)

crēdō, -ere, crēdidī, crēditum (+ *dat.*) to believe, suppose, trust

Crētē, Crētēs, f. Crete, an island in the eastern Mediterranean Sea

crīmen, crīminis, n. accusation, charge, indictment

crūdēlis, -e cruel, bitter

culpa, -ae, f., fault

cum ... tum, *conj.* both ... and

cum, *conj.* when, since, although

cupīdō, cupīdinis, m. desire, eagerness

cupidus, -a, -um longing, desirous

cūr, *interrog. adv.* why?

cūra, -ae, f. care, concern, worry, pain, sorrow

currus, -ūs, m. chariot, triumphal chariot

curvāmen, curvāminis, n. curvature, arc

Cyprus, -ī, f. Cyprus, an island sacred to the goddess Aphrodite/Venus

D

Daedalus, -ī, m. The mythical inventor who built the labyrinth that imprisoned the Minotaur

damnōsus, -a, -um destructive, ruinous

Daulias, Dauliadis Daulian

Daunias, Dauniadis, f. Apulia, region of southeastern Italy

dēbellō (1) to exhaust through war, crush

dēbeō, -ēre, dēbuī, dēbitum to be under an obligation, owe

dēcēdō, -ere, dēcessī, dēcessum to abandon, leave, withdraw

dēcernō, -ere, dēcrēvī, dēcrētum to settle, decide

dēcertō (1) (+ *dat.*) to contend with

decor, decōris, m. beauty

dēcrētum, -ī, n. decision, decree

dēdō, dēdere, dēdidī, dēditum to devote, give up

dēdūcō, -ere, dēdūxī, dēductum to adapt

dēficiō, -ere, dēfēcī, dēfectum to fail, run out

dēfugiō, -ere, dēfūgī to avoid

dēiciō, -ere, dēiēcī, dēiectum to cast down

dēlectō (1) to please, delight

Dēlos, -ī, f. a small (two square miles) island in the Aegean revered as the birthplace of Apollo and Diana

dēmissus, -a, -um low, close to the ground

dēmittō, -ere, -mīsī, -missum to send down, let fall, drop, lower

dēnique, *adv.* finally

dēpellō, -ere, dēpulī, dēpulsum to drive off, rebut, repel

dēscendō, -ere, -scendī, -scēnsum to fall, stoop, resort to, lower oneself

dēscrībō, -ere, dēscripsī, dēscriptum to mark out, map

dēserō, -ere, dēseruī, dēsertum to abandon, desert

dēspiciō, -ere, dēspexī, dēspectum to look down on

dētrahō, -ere, dētrāxī, dētrāctum to drag down, drag off

deus, -ī, m. god

dēvoveō, -ēre, dēvōvī, devōtum to curse

dicō (1) to dedicate, give oneself

dictum, -ī, n. word

dignitās, dignitātis, f. worth, reputation, authority

dīligēns, dīligentis careful, strict

dīmidium, -(i)ī, n. one-half

dīmittō, -ere, dīmīsī, dīmissum to let go, send away

dirimō, -ere, dirēmī, dirēmptum to pull apart, separate, break up

discessus, -ūs, m. departure, separation

discidium, -(i)ī, n. a tearing apart, a breakup

disciplīna, -ae, f. education, knowledge, doctrine, system

discō, -ere, didicī to learn, know

discrīmen, discrīminis, n. distinction, difference

dispār, disparis unequal, dissimilar

disputō (1) to dispute, discuss, argue

dissociābilis, -e incompatible

distō (1) to stand apart

dīva, -ae, f. goddess

dīvīnus, -a, -um holy, divine

dō, dare, dedī, datum to allow, give

dolor, dolōris, m. grief, pain, passion, anger

dolus, -ī, m. trick

druidēs, druidum, m. pl. Druids

dūcō, -ere, duxī, ductum to lead, draw (out)

dulcis, -e sweet, dear, fond

dum, *conj.* while, until

duo, duae, duo, *card. num. adj.* two

dūrus, -a, -um hard(y), harsh, stern

E

eburnus, -a, -um (of) ivory

ēdiscō, -ere, ēdidicī to learn thoroughly or by heart

efferō, efferre, extulī, ēlātum to bring forth, to carry out, to set out, to raise

effingō, -ere, effixī, effixum to express, portray

ēgregius, -a, -um extraordinary, distinguished, uncommon

elephantus, -ī, m. elephant, ivory

ēmittō, -ere, ēmīsī, ēmissum to send forth, hurl

ēnervis, -e weakened, enfeebled

enim, *adv.* indeed, for

ēnō (1) to swim out, fly forth

ēnsis, ēnsis, m. sword

eō, īre, iī (īvī), ītum to go

eō, *adv.* there

Eōus, -a, -um eastern (*lit.* of Eos, goddess of the dawn)

epistula (epistola), -ae, f. letter

eques, equitis, m. cavalryman, knight, man of equestrian rank

equidem, *adv.* indeed, truly, surely

ergō, *adv.* therefore, then, consequently

ēripiō, -ere, -ripuī, -reptum to snatch away

errō (1) to wander

error, errōris, m. wandering

ērudiō, -īre, ērudīvī, ērudītum to teach, instruct

exanimō (1) to kill

excellō, -ere, excelluī (+ *abl.*) to excel in, be superior in

excipiō, excipere, excēpī, exceptum to accept, receive

excitō (1) to arouse, rouse, inspire; call up, stir up

excūdō, -ere, excūdī, excūsum to hammer out, fashion

exercitus, -ūs, m. army

exilium, -(i)ī, n. exile, banishment

exīstimō (1) to consider, judge, think

exitus, -ūs, m. exit, outlet, egress

expediō, -īre, expedīvī, expedītum to free, extricate, release

expellō, -ere, -pulī, -pulsum to drive out, expel

experior, experīrī, expertus sum to make a trial of, try out; to know from experience

exsistō, -ere, exstitī to come forth, appear, to prove to be, to show oneself

exstinguō, -ere, exstīnxī, exstīnctum to quench, destroy, extinguish

extrēma, -ōrum, n. pl. end, death, funeral

extrēmus, -a, -um furthest

F

fābulōsus, -a, -um legendary, storied

facilis, -e easy, favorable, ready

facinus, facinoris, n. crime

falsus, -a, -um false, deceitful, mock

fāma, -ae, f. story, fame

familiāris, -e familiar, intimate

familiāris, familiaris, m./f. friend

familiāritās, familiāritātis, f. friendship, intimacy, familiarity

fās, n. *indecl.* right, divine law

febris, febris, f. fever, disease

fēcundus, -a, -um fertile, fruitful

fēlīx, fēlīcis, *adj.* happy, fortunate, lucky

fēmina, -ae, f. woman, wife

ferē, *adv.* nearly, almost, usually

feriō, -īre to hit, strike, blow; kill

ferō, ferre, tulī, lātum to bring, bear, carry

ferrum, -ī, n. sword

fidēs, fideī, f. faith, honor, pledge

fīgō, -ere, fīxī, fīxum to fasten, fix, pierce

fīlum, -ī, n. thread, string

fīnis, fīnis, m. end; pl. boundary

fistula, -ae, f. pipe, panpipe

flāvus, -a, -um yellow

flectō, -ere, flexī, flextum to bend, twist

flōs, flōris, m. flower

fluō, -ere, flūxī, fluxum to flow

foedus, foederis, n. agreement, treaty; bond, contract

fōns, fontis, m. spring, fountain, source

foris, foris, f. door

forma, -ae, f. form, beauty, shape, appearance

fors, fortis, f. chance

fragilis, -e easily destroyed, fragile

frāternus, -a, -um of or pertaining to a brother, fraternal

fraus, fraudis, f. theft

fretum, -ī, n. strait; (in pl.) the sea

frōns, frontis, f. front, forehead, brow

frūstrā, *adv.* in vain

fulg(e)ō, -ēre (-ere), fulsī to shine, gleam, glitter

fulmen, fulminis, n. thunderbolt

fundāmentum, -ī, n. basis

fundus, -ī, m. estate

fūnus, fūneris, n. funeral, death, disaster

furor, furōris, m. madness, frenzy

fūrtum, -ī, n. theft, secret action, trick

Fūscus, -ī, m. Aristius Fuscus

G

Gabīnius, -ī, m. Aulus Gabinius; Gabinius had been a strong supporter of Pompey and had served as one of his officers, but during the Civil Wars he supported Caesar

Gallicus, -a, -um of Gaul

Gallus, -a, -um Gallic, Gaul

garritus, -ūs, m. chattering

gaudeō, -ēre, gāvīsus sum (+ *abl.*) to rejoice in

gelidus, -a, -um cold

geminus, -a, -um twin

gena, -ae, f. cheek

generō (1) to produce, create

gēns, gentis, f. race, clan, family, people, nation

genus, generis, n. origin, family, class, type; offspring

gerō, -ere, gessī, gestum to wage, wear

glōria, -ae, f. honor, distinction

Gnōsius, -a, -um of Knossos, the chief city of Crete

gradior, gradī, gressus sum to go, journey

gradus, -ūs, m. step, gait, pace, stride

grātia, -ae, f. charm, grace, influence, favor

grātus, -a, -um pleasing

gravidus, -a, -um heavy, laden, weighed down

gravis, -e heavy, serious, severe

gravō (1) to weigh down

grex, gregis, m. herd, flock

guttur, -is, n. throat

H

habeō, -ēre, habuī, habitum to have; (in the passive) be considered

Hadria, -ae, f. the Adriatic Sea

haereō, -ēre, haesī, haesum (+ *dat.*) to cling to

harundō, harundinis, f. a reed, sharpened reed, arrow

haud, *adv.* hardly, scarcely

Helicē, Helicēs, f. the Greek name for the constellation Ursa Major

Herculeus, -a, -um of Hercules

hērēditās, hērēditātis, f. inheritance

hērōs, hērōis, m. hero, mighty warrior

heu, *interj.* alas

hīc, *adv.* here

honestum, -ī, n. virtue, honesty, sincerity

honōs, honōris, m. mark of honor, office; honor, esteem

horridus, -a, -um rough, scruffy, unkempt

hortor (1) to urge, encourage

hospitium, -(i)ī, n. hospitality, guest-host relationship

hūc, *adv.* here, to this place

humilis, -e slight

Hyadēs, -um, f. the Hyades, a cluster of 5 stars in the constellation Taurus

Hydaspēs, Hydaspis, m. Hydaspes, tributary of river Indus

Hyrcanī, -ōrum, m. pl. people living on the shores of the Caspian Sea

I

iaculum, -ī, n. javelin

Īapetus, -ī, m. the Titan Iapetus

Īāpyx (3 syllables), **Īāpygis,** m. north-by-northwest wind

ibi, *adv.* there, then

Īcarus, -ī, m. Icarus, Daedalus's son

īdem, eadem, idem the same

identidem, *adv.* continually, again and again

ideō, *adv.* on that account, therefore, for that reason

igitur, *adv.* therefore

ignārus, -a, -um unaware

ignis, ignis, m. fire, heat of the sun

ignōtus, -a, -um unknown

īlia, īlium, n. pl., groin, loins

imāgō, imāginis, f. image, likeness

imitor (1) to imitate

immānis, -e huge, immense

immō, *adv.* on the contrary, no indeed

immolō (1) to sacrifice

immūnitās, immūnitātis, f. immunity, exception

impediō, -īre, -īvī, -ītum to hinder, impede

imperium, -(i)ī, n. command

impius, -a, -um impious, wicked, irreverent

impōnō, -ere, imposuī, impositum to place on, impose, establish

impudīcus, -a, -um immoral, indecent

īmus, -a, -um lowest, bottom

incestus, -a, -um unholy, profane; unchaste, lewd

incidō, -ere, incidī, incasum to fall in, happen, occur

incipiō, -ere, incēpī, inceptum to begin, undertake

incolumis, -e safe, sound, unharmed

incommodum, -ī, n. disadvantage, misfortune, harm

incumbō, -ere, incubuī, incubitum (+ *dat.*) to oppress, settle, weigh upon

inde, *adv.* from there

Indī, Indōrum, m. pl. the inhabitants of India

inermis, -e unarmed

inextrīcābilis, -e impossible to find one's way out

infāmis, -e ill-famed, disreputable

infēlīx, infēlicis unhappy, miserable, poor

inferī, inferōrum, n. pl. the dead; regions the dead inhabit

inferō, -ferre, -tulī, illātum to bring forward, produce, introduce

inferus, -a, -um lower, infernal

ingrātus, -a, -um unpleasing

ingredior, ingredī, ingressus sum to step, stride, enter

inimīcus, -a, -um unfriendly, hostile

inīquus, -a, -um unjust, harsh, uneven

iniūria, -ae, f. wrongdoing, oppression, injury

innītor, innītī, innīxus sum (+ *abl.*) to lean on, rest on

innocēns, innocentis harmless, innocent

īnsignis, -e distinguished, marked, noteworthy

īnsomnium, -(i)ī, n. dream, vision

īnspērāns, īnspērantis not expecting or hoping

īnstar, n. *indecl.* likeness, presence, weight, dignity

īnstituō, -ere, īnstituī, īnstitūtum to put in place, establish, build

īnstruō, -ere, īnstruxī, īnstructum to equip, provide

īnsuētus, -a, -um unaccustomed

īnsum, inesse, īnfuī to be in or on

integer, integra, integrum whole, untouched, upright

interdīcō, -ere, interdīxī, interdictum to banish (someone) from

intereā, *adv.* meanwhile

intereō, interīre, interiī/ivī, interitum to die

interpretor (1) to interpret, explain

intersum, interesse, interfuī (+ *dat.*) to take part in, attend to

intestīnum, -ī, n. intestines

invītus, -a, -um unwilling, reluctant

ipse, ipsa, ipsum, *demonstrative pron.* and *adj.*, self, very

iste, ista, istud, *demonstrative pron.* and *adj.*, that

ita, *adv.* so, such

iter, itineris, n. journey

iterum, *adv.* again

Itylus, -ī, m. Itylus

Iuba, -ae, m. Juba, Juba I, Numidian king who supported Pompey in the civil war

iubeō, -ēre, iussī, iussum to order

iūcundus, -a, -um pleasant

iūdex, iūdicis, m. judge

iūdicium, -(i)ī, n. trial, decision

Iūnōnius, -a, -um of or pertaining to Juno

Iuppiter, Iovis, m. Jupiter, the king of the gods

iūrgium, -(i)ī, n. altercation, quarrel, shouting match

iūrō (1) to swear (by), take an oath

iūs, iūris, n. right, law

iussum, -ī, n. command, order, behest

iuvencus, -ī, m. bull calf; steer

iuvenis, iuvenis, m./f. youth, young (man, woman)

iuventa, -ae, f. youth

iuventūs, iuventūtis, f. youth, young people

iuxtā, *adv.* near, next, *prep. + acc.* close to

L

lābor, lābī, lāpsus sum to slide, slip, fall

lacertus, -ī, m. arm

laetus, -a, -um happy

laevus, -a, -um left, left hand

Lalagē, Lalagēs, f., Lalage, woman's name; Greek for "chatterer."

lambō, -ere, lambī to lick, wash

languidus, -a, -um exhausted

lateō, -ēre, latuī to escape the notice of, be unknown to

latrōcinium, -(i)ī, n. robbery, banditry

lātus, -a, -um wide

latus, lateris, n. side, extreme part or region, flank, lungs, body

laus, laudis, f. praise, fame, glory

Lebinthos, -ī, f. an island in the Sporadic chain, off the east coast of mainland Greece

lēgātiō, lēgātiōnis, f. embassy, mission

lēniō, -īre, lēnīvī, lēnītum to soften, soothe, calm

lēnis, -e gentle

lētum, -ī, n. death, destruction

levis, -e light

levō (1) to raise up, lift

līberāliter, *adv.* generously, kindly

līberius, *comparative adv.* too freely

libīdō, libīdinis, f. desire, passion

lībō (1) to drink

lībrō (1) to level, balance

licet, licēre, *impers. verb,* it is permitted

līmen, līminis, n. doorway, threshold

līmes, līmitis, m. path, road, course

linquō, -ere, liquī to leave

līnum, -ī, n. thread, string

litterae, -ārum, f. pl. writing

lītus, lītoris, n. shore

locus, -ī, m. rank, position, place

longē, *adv.* (from) afar, at a distance, far and wide

loquāx, loquācis talkative

loquor, loquī, locūtus sum to talk

lūcidus, -a, -um clear, bright shining

lūna, -ae, f. moon, moonlight

lupus, -ī, m. wolf

lūsus, -ūs, m. play, sport

M

maciēs, maciēī, f. leanness, wasting disease

madeō, -ēre, maduī to grow wet

Maecēnas, Maecēnātis, m. Maecenas was the patron of Horace as well as of Vergil

magis, *adv.* more, rather

maledictum, -ī, n. slander, curse

mālō, mālle, māluī to prefer

malum, -ī, n. misfortune, harm

mandō (1) to entrust, commit

Mānēs, Mānium, m. (souls of) the dead, Hades

manus, -ūs, f. hand

Mārcellus, -ī, m. 1. Marcus Claudius Marcellus, d. 208 BCE; famous Roman consul, served in both the First and Second Punic Wars; was an outstanding general in the Second Punic War, and was an ancestor of the younger Marcellus 2. Marcus Claudius Marcellus, 42–23 BCE; son of Octavia, sister of Augustus, and first husband of Augustus's daughter Julia

mare, maris, n. sea

marmor, marmoris, n. marble

Marpēs(s)ius, -a, -um of Marpe(s)sus

mātrimōnium, -(i)ī, n. matrimony, wedlock

Maurus, -a, -um Moorish, African

maximē, *adv.* especially

maximus, -a, -um largest, greatest

meātus, -ūs, m. course, path, motion

medius, -a, -um middle

mel, mellis, n. honey

melior, melius better, superior, finer

membrum, -ī, n. limb, part

memorō (1) to mention, recount, relate

mēnsis, mēnsis, m. month

metus, -ūs, m. fear

mīlitia, -ae, f. the military, military service

minimus, -a, -um smallest, littlest, least

Mīnōïus, -a, -um of Minos

Mīnōs, Mīnōis, m. Minos, king of Crete

minus, *adv.* less

mīrābilis, -e wonderful, wondrous

mīror (1) to admire, wonder

misceō, -ēre, miscuī, mixtum to mix

miser, misera, miserum unhappy, wretched

miseror (1) to pity, commiserate

mittō, -ere, mīsī, missum to send

modo . . . modo, *adv.* now . . . now, at one time . . . at another

modo, *adv.* recently

modus, -ī, m. way, mode

moechus, -ī, m. adulterer

mōlēs, molis, f. mass, burden

molliō, -īre, mollīvī, mollitum to soften, weaken

mollis, -e soft, gentle, graceful, effeminate

monimentum, -ī, n. trophy, testimonial, monument

monitus, -ūs, m. warning, admonition

monumentum, -ī, n. monument, remembrance, reminder

morbus, -ī, m. sickness, disease

mordeō, mordēre, momordī, morsum to bite, sting, vex, attack

mortuus, -a, -um dead, deceased

mōs, mōris, m. custom, usage, rule, law

mōtus, -ūs, m. motion, movement

muliēbris, -e womanly, of a woman

mulier, mulieris, f. woman

mundus, -ī, m. world, universe

mūniō, -īre, -īvī, -ītum to fortify; *(of roads)* build

N

nam, *conj.* for

namque, *conj.* for

nātālis, -e of birth, native

nātiō, nātiōnis, f. nation, race, people

nātīvus, -a, -um native

nātus, -ī, m. son, child

nāvicula, -ae, f. small vessel, skiff

nebula, -ae, f. cloud, mist, fog

nec, *conj.* and . . . not

necō (1) to kill

nefandus, -a, -um unspeakable, evil

nefās (indeclinable) wickedness, something forbidden by or hateful to the gods

neglegō, -ere, neglēxī, neglēctum to disregard

nemus, nemoris, n. (sacred) grove, forest

nepōs, nepōtis, m. grandson; descendant

neque . . . neque, *conj.* neither . . . nor

neque, *conj.* and . . . not, nor

nēquīquam, *adv.* in vain

nēve, *adv.* and not

nīdus, -ī, m. nest

nīl, n. nothing

Nīlus, -ī, m. Nile river

nimium, *adv.* too, too much, very

nisi, *conj.* unless, if not, except

nitēns, nitentis gleaming, bright, shining

nix, nivis, f. snow

nōbilis, -e known; noble, of noble birth

nōmen, nōminis, n. name

nōscō, -ere, nōvī, nōtum to learn, recognize, know

noster, nostra, nostrum of ours, our

nōta, -ae, f. mark, sign

nōtitia, -ae, f. acquaintance

nōtus, -a, -um, well-known, notorious

Notus, -ī, m. south wind

novō (1) to make new, change

noxia, -ae, f. harm, crime

nūbilum, -ī, n. cloud, cloudiness

nūbō, -ere, nūpsī, nūptum to marry

nūllus, -a, -um no, none

nūmen, nūminis, n. divine will, divine power, divinity

numerus, -ī, m. account, number, rhythm, meter

numquam, *adv.* never

nuntiō (1) to announce, speak

nuntius, -(i)ī, m. messenger, message

nūper, *adv.* not long ago, lately, recently

nūtrīx, nūtricis, f. nurse, especially a wet-nurse

O

obiūrgō (1) to scold, chide, blame, upbraid

obscūrus, -a, -um dark, obscure, dim

obstipescō, -ere, obstipuī to be amazed, astonished

obstringō, -ere, obstrinxī, obstrictum to hold in check, confine

obstruō, -ere obstruxī, obstructum to block, close

ōdium, -(i)ī, n. hatred

odōrātus, -a, -um fragrant, scented

officium, -(i)ī, n. duty

ōlim, *adv.* once, some day

omnis, -e all

opēs, opium, f. power, resources

opifex, opificis, m. craftsman, artisan

opīmus, -a, -um rich, splendid, sumptuous

optingō, -ere, optigī to happen, occur

optō (1) to desire, wish

opus, operis, n. work, toil

ōrdō, ōrdinis, m. row, order, position

Ōrīōn, Ōrīonis, m. the constellation in the South known as the Hunter

ornāmentum, -ī, n. ornament, badge, distinction, mark

ōrō (1) to pray (for), entreat, plead, argue

ōs, ōris, n. mouth, face

ōsculum, -ī, n. kiss

P

pāgus, -ī, m. village, a country district

palam, *adv.* in the open, in public

pār, paris equal

parcō, -ere, pepercī (parsī) (+ *dat.*) to spare

pareō, -ēre, paruī (+ *dat.*) to obey

pariter, *adv.* at the same time, together

parō (1) to get ready, prepare

Paros, -ī, f. an island in the Aegean

Parthī, -ōrum, m. pl. Parthians; people living in Parthia, a land northeast of Syria

parum, *adv.* slightly, too little, not

Pāsiphaē, Pāsiphaēs, f. Pasiphae

pāstor, pāstōris, m. shepherd

pateō, -ēre, patuī to be open, accessible

paternus, -a, -um of or pertaining to a father, paternal

patior, patī, passus sum to allow, permit

patria, -ae, f. fatherland, homeland

patrius, -a, -um of a father, paternal

patruus, -ī, m. uncle

paucī, paucae, pauca few

paulātim, *adv.* gradually, little by little

pāx, pācis, f. pact, treaty; peace, quiet, repose

pectus, pectoris, n. chest, heart

pecus, pecudis, f. sheep

pelagus, -ī, n. sea

pellō, -ere, pulsī, pulsum to pluck

pendeō, -ēre, pependī to hang

pendō, -ere, pependī, pēnsum to pay

penetrō (1) to make one's way to

penna, -ae, f. feather

per, *prep.* + *acc.* through, because of

percipiō, -ere, percēpī, perceptum to catch, secure

perdiscō, -ere, perdidicī to learn thoroughly, learn by heart

perdūcō, -ere, perdūxī, perductum to maintain

perficiō, -ere, perfēcī, perfectum to finish, make

perītus, -a, -um skilled, experienced

perlegō, -ere, perlēgī, perlēctum to scan, survey

permaneō, -ēre, permansī, permānsum to remain

perōdī, perōdisse, perōsum to despise, loathe

perpetior, perpetī, perpessus sum to tolerate; to dare

perpetuus, -a, -um forever

perrumpō, -ere, perrūpī, perruptum to break through

persōna, -ae, f. person, individual

persuādeō, -ēre, persuāsī, persuāsum (+ *dat.*) to convince, persuade

perturbō (1) to disturb

perūrō, -ere, perussī, perustum to burn through and through, consume

pēs, pedis, m. foot; step

pestis, pestis, m. a deadly disease, plague, bane

petō, -ere, petīvī, petītum to seek, attempt, ask

petulāns, petulantis, impudent

pharētra, -ae, f., quiver

Phoenissa, -ae, f. Phoenician (woman), Dido

piger, pigra, pigrum lifeless, inactive, lazy

Pindarus, -ī, m. Pindar, the Greek lyric poet

pinna, -ae, f. wing

plācō (1) to calm, appease

plēbs, plēbis *or* **plēbēs, plēbeī,** f. the common people

plēnus, -a, -um full of, filled with

plērīque, plērōrumque, m. pl. the majority, most people

plērumque, *adv.* very often

plūma, -ae, f. feather

plūrimus, -a, -um most, very great, very many

plūs, plūris more, several

poena, -ae, f. punishment

Poenus, -a, -um Phoenician, Carthaginian

pollex, pollicis, m. thumb

Pompēius, Pompēī, m. Pompey (the Great)

pōnō, -ere, posuī, positum to build, place, lay aside, make quiet

pōpulētum, -ī, n. plantation or stand of poplar trees

populus, -ī, m. people, nation

porta, -ae, f. gate

portentum, -ī, n. monster, portent, abnormal phenomenon

poscō, -ere, poposcī to demand, require

posteā, *adv.* afterwards

posterī, -ōrum, m. pl. coming generations, posterity

postquam, *conj.* after

potēns, potentis powerful

potentia, -ae, f. force, power

potestās, potestātis, f. power, authority

pōtiō, pōtiōnis, f. a drink, potion

praeceps, praecipitis rushing, headlong

praeceptum, -ī, n. lesson, command, instruction, rule

praedicō (1) to allege

praedō, praedōnis, m. pirate

praemittō, -ere, praemīsī, praemissum to send ahead

praemium, -ī, n. reward

praepes, praepetis swift

praesidium, -(i)ī, n. help, assistance, protection

praesum, praeesse, praefuī, praefutūrum to preside over, be in charge of

praeter, *prep. + acc.* except

praetereā, *adv.* besides, moreover

praetereō, praeterīre, praeterīvī, praeteritum to pass, go past

prātum, -ī, n. meadow

precor (1) pray, beg

premō, -ere, pressī, pressum to suppress, press hard

pretium, -(i)ī, n. price, cost

prīnceps, prīncipis, m. most eminent, chief, prince

prīncipātus, -ūs, m. leadership, rule, first place

prīscus, -a, -um old, ancient, of yesteryear

prīstinus, -a, -um ancient, former

prius, *adv.* before, previously, first

prō (*prep. + abl.*) by virtue of, in return for

prōavus, -ī, m. great-grandfather

probō (1) to approve

prōcūrō (1) to attend to, administer

prōdūcō, -ere, prōdūxī, prōductum to induce

proelium, -(i)ī, n. battle, fight

profectō, *adv.* truly, really, certainly

proficīscor, proficīscī, profectus sum to set out

profundus, -a, -um deep, profound, vast

progeniēs, progeniēī, f. offspring, descendant

prōlēs, prōlis, f. child, offspring

prōmittō, -ere, prōmīsī, prōmissum to promise

prope, *adv.* nearly, almost

propinquus, -a, -um near, neighboring

propinquus, -ī, m. relative

prōpōnō, -ere, prōposuī, prōpositum to propose, suggest

propriē, *adv.* properly, particularly

propter, *prep. + acc.* because of, on account of

prōpulsō (1) to drive off, repel

prōsequor, prōsequī, prōsecūtus sum to follow, attend, escort

prōtinus, *adv.* successively

prūdēns, prudentis wise

Ptolemaeus, -ī, m. Ptolemy

pūblicē, *adv.* on behalf of the state, as a community, publicly

putō (1) to think, suppose, consider

Q

quaerō, -ere, quaesīvī, quaesītum to seek

quaestiō, quaestiōnis, f. a seeking; investigation, judicial inquiry

quālis, -e of what sort, what kind of

quam, *adv.* how, than

quamdiū, *interrog. and rel. adv.* how long?; as long as, so long as, until

quantus, -a, -um how (much, great, many); as

quārē, *adv.* therefore

quatiō, -ere, quassī, quassum to shake, move

queō, quīre, quīvī (-iī), quītum to be able, can

quī, quae, quod, *relative pron.,* which, that

quīcumque, quaecumque, quodcumque whatever

quīdam, quaedam, quoddam, *indefinite pron. and adj.,* certain, a certain

Quirīnus, -ī, m. the deified Romulus as god of war

quisquam, quicquam, *pronoun,* anyone, anything

quisque, quidque, *pron.* each, each one, everybody

quondam, *adv.* once

quoque, *adv.* also, too

quotannīs, *adv.* annually, every year

R

rabiēs, rabieī, f. madness; fury

radius, -(i)ī, m. rod, spoke, compass

rāmus, -ī, m. branch

rapidus, -a, -um scorching, fierce

ratiō, ratiōnis, f. account, transaction, business

ratis, ratis, f. raft, boat

rebellis, -e rebellious, insurgent

recēns, recentis recent, fresh

recēnseō, -ēre, recēnsuī, recēnsum to count, review

recipiō, -ere, recēpī, receptum to receive

recreō (1) to recreate, restore, revive

reddō, -ere, reddidī, redditum to give back, restore, render

redux, reducis coming back, returning

referō, referre, rettulī, relātum to bring back, return

refugiō, -ere, refūgī to flee (away), withdraw, shun,

regiō, regiōnis, f. region, area

rēgius, -a, -um royal, regal

rēgnum, -ī, n. kingdom

regō, regere, rēxī, rēctum to rule, guide, direct

rēligiō, rēligiōnis, f. piety to the gods; (pl.) religious observances, religious matters

relinquō, -ere, relīquī, relictum to leave (behind), abandon

reliquus, -a, -um remaining, left over

rēmigium, -(i)ī, n. oars, wings

remissus, -a, -um relaxed

remittō, -ere, remīsī, remissum to relax, loosen, release

renīdeō, -ēre to smile with pleasure, beam

reperiō, -īre, repperī, repertum to find, discover

repetō, -ere, repetīvī, repetītum to return, to trace back

requīrō, -ere, requīsīvī, requīsītum to look for, ask for

rēs, reī, f. thing

resolvō, -ere, resolvī, resolūtum to solve

resonō (1) to resound, echo

respectō (1) to look back upon

respiciō, -ere, respexī, respectum to look at, look back at

respondeō, -ēre, respondī, respōnsum to answer, sympathize with; balance

restituō, -ere, restituī, restitūtum to restore

revīsō, revisere to revisit, see again

Rhēnus, -ī, m. the Rhine, a river that separates Gaul from Germany

Rhodopē, Rhodopēs, f. a mountain range in Thrace

rīdeō, -ēre, rīsī, rīsum to laugh

rōbur, rōboris, n. oak tree, oak wood; strength

Rōmānus, -a, -um Roman, of Rome

rumpō, -ere, rūpī, ruptum to break, tear, burst

ruō, -ere, ruī to rush

rūpes, rupis, f. cliff

rūrsus *or* **rūrsum,** *adv.* back, backwards; on the other hand, then again

S

sacerdōs, sacerdōtis, m. or f. priest, priestess

sacrificium, -(i)ī, n. sacrifice

sacrō (1) to dedicate

sacrum, -ī, n. (in pl.) rituals

saeculum, -ī, n. age

Sagae, -ārum, m. pl. Scythians

sagitta, -ae, f. arrow

sagittifer, sagittifera, sagittiferum arrow-bearing, carrying arrows

saliō, -īre, saluī, saltum to leap

Samos, -ī, f. an island in the eastern Mediterranean off the coast of Asia Minor between Ephesus and Miletus

sānctus, -a, -um holy

scelerātus, -a, -um criminal, outlawed

scelus, sceleris, n. wickedness, crime, affliction

secō, secāre, secuī, sectum to cut, cleave; pass through

sēdēs, sēdis, f. seat; foundation, support, basis

sēmōtus, -a, -um removed, distant

senīlis, -e old, aged

sentus, -a, -um rough, thorny

sepeliō, -īre, sepelīvī, sepultum to bury

septemgeminus, -a, -um sevenfold

septēnus, -a, -um seven each

sepulcrum, -ī, n. grave, tomb

sequester, sequestrī, m. third party acting as a depositary or escrow agent

sequor, sequī, secūtus sum to follow

sermō, sermōnis, m. conversation, speech

servō (1) to save, preserve

seu, conj. or

sevērus, -a, -um stern

sī tamen, conj. if indeed

Sibylla, -ae, f. ancient Italian prophetess

sīc, adv. thus, so

siccus, -a, -um dry, thirsty

sīcine, interrogatory adv. thus, so

sīdereus, -a, -um starry, heavenly

sīdus, sīderis, n. star, constellation, planet

silex, silicis, m./f. flint, rock, crag

simul, adv. together, at the same time, as soon as

simulācrum, -ī, n. likeness, image, representation

sincērē, adv. honestly, sincerely

singulāris, -e remarkable, extraordinary

singulī, -ae, -a each one, all these

sistō, -ere, stitī, statum to stop, to cause to stand firm

sitis, sitis, f. thirst

situs, -ūs, m. position; neglect; decay

sīve, conj. whether . . . or

sīve . . . sīve, conj. whether . . . or

sōl, sōlis, m. sun

soleō, -ēre, solitus sum to be used to, be accustomed to

sollicitō (1) to agitate, incite, bribe

solum, -ī, n. ground, soil, land

Somnus, -ī, m. Sleep, Slumber personified as a divinity

Sona, -ae, f. most probably the spring in Sarbiewski's ancestral home or village

sors, sortis, f. lot, destiny

spatium, -(i)ī, n. distance

spectāculum, -ī, n. sight, spectacle

spīrō (1) to breathe, blow, live, quiver

spolium, -(i)ī, n. spoil, booty, plunder

sponte, f. (abl. only) of one's own accord

statua, -ae, f. statue

sternō, -ere, strāvī, strātum to lay low, strew

stirps, stirpis, f. stock, lineage, race

stīva, -ae, f. the shaft of a plow handle

stō, stāre, stetī, statum to stand

strepitus, -ūs, m. uproar, noise, clamor

stringō, -ere, strinxī, strictum to unsheathe, draw

studeō, -ēre, studuī (+ *dat.*) to study, apply oneself to

stultitia, -ae, f. foolishness

subdūcō, -ere, subdūxī, subductum to steal, hide

subiciō, -ere, subiēcī, subiectum to vanquish

sublīmis, -e lifted up, raised up

subtrahō, -ere, subtrāxī, subtractum to withdraw

succēdō, -ere, successī, successum to advance, become a successor

succendō, -ere, succendī, succēnsum to set fire to, light

suffrāgium, -(i)ī, n. vote

summus, -a, -um highest

sūmō, -ere, sūmpsī, sūmptum to take

superbus, -a, -um proud, haughty

superēmineō, -ēre to tower above, surpass

superī, superōrum, m. pl. those above, the gods above

superō (1) to surpass, overcome; excel, outdo

supplicium, -ī, n. supplication, punishment, execution

suppōnō, -ere, supposuī, suppos(i)tum to join

surgō, -ere, surrēxī, surrēctum to rise

suscēnseō, -ēre, suscēnsuī (+ *dat.*) to be angry with, bear a grudge

suspendō, -ere, suspendī, suspēnsum to hang up

suus, -a, -um his, her, its, their

Sychaeus, -ī, m. deceased husband of Dido

Syrtis, Syrtis, f. Syrtis (especially plural), name of two areas of sandy flats on the coast between Carthage and Cyrene

T

tābescō, tābescere, tābuī to melt gradually

tālis, -e such

tam, *adv.* so, to that degree, to such a degree

tamen, *adv.* nevertheless, yet

tandem, *adv.* finally, at last

tangō, -ere, tetigī, tāctum to graze, touch

tantus, -a, -um so great, such great

tēctum, -ī, n. roof, house, home

tegō, -ere, tēxī, tēctum to protect

tellūs, tellūris, f. land, earth, country, ground

temerē, *adv.* heedlessly, recklessly

temeritās, temeritātis, f. rashness, recklessness, heedlessness

temptō (1) to try

tempus, temporis, n. time

teneō, -ēre, tenuī, tentum to hold

tener, tenera, tenerum tender, sensitive, fragile

terminus, -ī, m. boundary line, limit

tertius, -a, -um third

testis, testis, m./f. witness

testūdō, testūdinis, f. shell of a tortoise; lyre

Teucer, Teucrī, m. Trojan

Thrēicius, -a, -um Thracian

timeō, -ēre, timuī to fear, have cause to fear; be at risk from

tollō, -ere, sustulī, sublātum to raise up, excite

torvus, -a, -um fierce, grim, lowering

totidem, *indecl. adj.* just as many

tōtus, -a, -um whole, entire, all

tractō (1) to handle, manage

trādō, -ere, trādidī, trāditum to pass on, hand down, teach

trādūcō, -ere, trādūxī, trāductum to transfer, bring across, lead over

trahō, -ere, trāxī, tractum to drag, draw

trānsferō, trānsferre, trānstulī, trānslātum to carry across, transfer

trānsiliō, -īre to leap across, hasten through

trecentī, trecentae, trecenta three hundred

tremulus, -a, -um trembling, quivering

tribūnus, tribūnī, m. tribune, one of ten officials elected annually by the plebeians for the protection of their rights

tribūtum, -ī, n. tribute, tax

triplex, triplicis triple, i.e., very strong

tristis, -e sad

triumphō (1) to have a triumphal procession

Trivia, -ae, f. *lit.* "she of the fork in the road," an epithet of the goddess Diana

Trōius, -a, -um Trojan, of Troy

trux, trucis savage, cruel

tueor, tuērī, tuitus (tūtus) sum to look (at), watch

tumultus, -ūs, m. tumult, uprising, clamor

tunc, *adv.* then

tundō, -ere, tutudī, tūnsum to buffet, to beat repeatedly

turbidus, -a, -um turbulent

turbō (1) to confuse, shake, disturb

turpis, -e disgraceful

Tuscus, -a, -um Etruscan

U

ultimus, -a, -um last, farthest, at the edge of

ultrā, *prep. + acc.* beyond

umbrifer, umbrifera, umbriferum shady; shade-bearing

umerus, -ī, m. shoulder

umquam, *adv.* ever

ūnā, *adv.* at the same time, together

unda, -ae, f. wave, sea

undique, *adv.* everywhere

urbānus, -a, -um refined, sophisticated, suave

urgeō, -ēre, ursī to press, push, drive

usque, *adv.* as far as one can go, continuously, constantly

usus, -ūs, m. use, need

ut, utī, *conj.* so that, that, as, when

ūtor, ūtī, ūsus sum (+ *abl.*) to use

ūtrum, *adv.* whether

V

vacātiō, vacātiōnis, f. exemption

vacuus, -a, -um empty

vadum, -ī, n. ford; (in pl.) the sea

vagor (1) to wander

vagus, -a, -um shifting, moving about

valeō, -ēre, valuī to be strong, be healthy, thrive

vātēs, vātis, m./f. bard, poet

-ve, *conj.* or

vel, *conj.* or

velut, *adv.* just as, even as, as

venēnātus, -a, -um poisonous

venēnum, venēnī, n. poison

vērē, *adv.* truly

versō (1) to engage; (in the passive) to be engaged in, take part in, be involved in, occupy oneself with

versus, -ūs, m. verse, line (of poetry)

vērus, -a, -um true, real, genuine, honest

Vestālis, -e of or pertaining to Vesta, goddess of the hearth (fireplace)

vestīgium, -(i)ī, n. step, walking

vetō, -āre, vetuī, vetitum to deny, forbid

vexō (1) to move violently, shake, agitate, harass

vīcīnia, -ae, f. nearness, proximity

videō, -ēre, vīdī, vīsum to see; (in passive) to seem

vīmen, vīminis, n. twig, basket

vinculum, -ī, n. chain, bond

virgō, virginis, f. maiden; virgin

virīlis, -e of a man, male

virtūs, virtūtis, f. excellence, virtue, manliness, courage

vīs, vīs, f. force, power, strength

vīsō, visēre, vīsī to go and see

vīta, -ae, f. life

vitium, -(i)ī, n. fault, flaw, vice

vītrum, -ī, n. glass

vīvō, -ere, vīxī, vīctum to live

vīvus, -a, -um living, alive, natural, lifelike

vix, *adv.* scarcely

volātus, -ūs, m. flying, flight

volō (1) to fly

voluntās, voluntātis, f. wish, will

voluptās, voluptātis, f. enjoyment, pleasure

voveō, -ēre, vōvī, vōtum to pledge, devote

vox, vōcis, f. voice, saying, word

vulgum, *adv.* (to) the general public

vulgus, -ī, n. crowd, public

vulnus, vulneris, n. wound, deadly blow

vultus, -ūs, m. countenance, face, aspect